I0428359

Informing the legislative debate since 1914 _____

U.S. Air Force Bomber Sustainment and Modernization: Background and Issues for Congress

Jeremiah Gertler
Specialist in Military Aviation

June 4, 2014

Congressional Research Service

7-5700

www.crs.gov

R43049

Summary

The United States' existing long-range bomber fleet of B-52s, B-1s, and B-2s are at a critical point in their operational life span. With the average age of each airframe being 50, 28, and 20 years old, respectively, military analysts are beginning to question just how long these aircraft can physically last and continue to be credible weapon systems. As potential adversaries acquire 21st century defense systems designed to prevent U.S. access to the global commons (sea, air, space, and cyberspace) and to limit U.S. forces' freedom of action within an operational area, the ability of these Cold War era bombers to get close enough to targets to be effective will continue to deteriorate. Although the Air Force is committed to the development and acquisition of its proposed Long-Range Strike-Bomber (LRS-B), it is anticipated that flight-testing of the new bomber will not start until the mid-2020s, with initial operational capability near 2030. With this timeline in mind, the Air Force has extended the operational lives of the B-52 and B-1 out to 2040 and the B-2 out to 2058. Air Force and aerospace industry experts insist that with sufficient funding for sustainment and modernization over their expected lifespans, all three of the existing bombers can physically last and continue to remain credible weapon systems. However, appropriations decisions made by Congress based on required military capabilities to meet national security objectives will ultimately determine how long the B-52, B-1, and B-2 will remain in service.

The central issue for Congress is how much funding should be appropriated for the continued sustainment and modernization of the B-52, B-1, and B-2 bombers over the remainder of their service lives. Interest in this subject stems from Congress's authority to approve, reject, or modify Air Force funding requests for bomber sustainment and modernization as well as its oversight of the nation's long-range strike requirements and capabilities. In addition, sustainment, modernization, and size of the bomber force have been perennial legislative topics since the early 1990s. As the Air Force progresses through development and acquisition of the LRS-B and begins the gradual phase-out of 50-year-old bombers, it is anticipated Congress will continue dealing with bomber sustainment and modernization legislation. Congress's decisions on appropriations for the bomber force could affect the nation's long-range strike capabilities and have unintended consequences on U.S. national security as well as the U.S. aerospace industry.

The context through which Congress will make these decisions includes U.S. national security and defense strategies and the expectation of the role the B-52, B-1, and B-2 will play in executing those strategies. Some of the many global and strategic variables that could become central in Congress's decision making on the bomber force include the following:

- the Obama Administration's 2012 rebalance in national security strategy toward the Asia-Pacific region and the military implications applicable to the bomber force;

- the expected contribution of bombers in accomplishing the critical missions of U.S. forces as outlined in the Department of Defense's strategic guidance, *Sustaining U.S. Global Leadership: Priorities for the 21st Century Defense*;

- the effectiveness and sustainability of the Air Force's continuous bomber presence operation—based in the Pacific at Anderson Air Force Base, Guam—and corresponding displays of worldwide power projection missions by all three bombers;

- the anti-access/area denial (A2/AD) challenge presented by potential adversaries and the developments related to bombers' employment in an A2/AD threat environment; and

- the bombers' role in nuclear deterrent operations and the impact of the New Strategic Arms Reduction Treaty on the B-52 and B-2.

The starting point for Congress's debate on bomber modernization and sustainment is the existing Air Force bomber force, which includes

- 76 B-52H Stratofortress bombers capable of both conventional and nuclear operations and capable of employing long-range standoff weapons. The B-52H first entered service on May 9, 1961.

- 63 B-1B Lancer bombers capable of supersonic and low-level flight, conventional only operations, and employing long-range standoff weapons. The B-1B became operational in 1986.

- 20 B-2A Spirit, low observable (stealth) bombers capable of both conventional and nuclear operations. The B-2A entered service in December 1993 and became fully operational capable (FOC) on December 17, 2003.

Potential congressional oversight and appropriations concerns for the sustainment and modernization of the U.S. Air Force's bomber force may include the following:

- the potential for a shortfall in the nation's long-range strike capabilities as development of the Air Force's proposed LRS-B continues;

- the feasibility and affordability of Air Force bomber sustainment and modernization plans and whether those plans bridge any potential long-range strike capabilities gap until the LRS-B becomes operational;

- the amount of money Congress and the nation should continue spending on 28- and 50-year-old bombers;

- the sufficiency of acquisition plans for the 80 to 100 LRS-Bs to backfill U.S. long-range strike requirements as the legacy bomber force ages out of service;

- the possibility of further delaying development and acquisition of the proposed LRS-B given sufficient levels of funding for sustainment and modernization of the current bomber force;

- the modernization, sustainment, and development of the weapons employed by the bomber force that affect the bombers' effectiveness and ability to operate in advanced, 21st century A2/AD threat environment;

- the potential implications of reduced bomber sustainment and modernization, and subsequent diminishing numbers of airframes, on any future rounds of base realignment and closure efforts; and

- the ability of the nation's industrial base to sustain an aging bomber force.

Contents

Figures

Tables

Appendixes

Contacts

Introduction

The central issue addressed by this report is how much Congress should consider appropriating for the continued sustainment and modernization of the B-52, B-1, and B-2 bombers over the remainder of their service lives. Many military experts note the advanced age of the United States' long-range bomber fleet. The B-52H Stratofortress, B-1B Lancer, and B-2A Spirit are now about 50, 28, and 20 years old respectively. In fact, Air Force Global Strike Command declared 2012 the "Year of the B-52" in honor of the 50th anniversary of the last delivery of a B-52 and the 60th anniversary of the first test flight of the YB-52.[1] The B-1B celebrated its 25th anniversary in 2010. The last B-2 delivery was in 1997. Although the Department of Defense and the Air Force are committed to the development and fielding of a new Long-Range Strike-Bomber (LRS-B), flight-testing of the new bomber will likely not start until the mid-2020s. Initial development of the B-2 began in the early 1980s and the first aircraft was delivered on December 17, 1993. If the B-2 experience is the norm, potential delivery of the first operational LRS-B may be expected sometime in the 2030 timeframe. With this in mind, can the U.S. Air Force's B-52Hs, B-1Bs, and B-2As physically last and continue to be credible weapon systems until the LRS-B is fielded? More importantly, does the nation's "legacy" bomber force possess the capabilities required to meet national security strategy objectives, especially in the face of potential adversaries possessing advanced, 21st century anti-access/area-denial (A2/AD) weapon systems?[2] The U.S. Air Force and aerospace industry's answer is "yes," provided sufficient sustainment and modernization funding is available over the remaining lifespan of these weapon systems.

Without sufficient sustainment and modernization funding, many analysts argue the U.S. bomber fleet will quickly become a decrepit force ill-suited to the potential challenges posed by 21st century adversaries. The average age of the bomber force is 33. Because of the physical wear-and-tear placed on these aircraft from the demands of military flight—compounded by 11 years of continuous combat—aging airframe structures need reinforcement, engines need to be replaced, and computer and electronic components need upgrading. Even if corrosion, metal fatigue, and parts obsolescence do not take their toll on the fleet, military analysts point out that potential adversaries are acquiring advanced, A2/AD weapon systems that would make it harder for the bombers to reach their targets, thus relegating them to a "standoff" weapons employment role.[3] But even "standoff" weapons have their limits, especially against deeply buried and/or hardened targets found in places like North Korea and Iran. Consequently, most experts agree all three bombers are in need of upgrades to their systems in order to counter A2/AD-equipped adversaries and require constant operational research and testing to evaluate and incorporate new and modern weapons into their arsenal.

---

[1] The YB-52 was the second B-52 prototype aircraft built. The aircraft was completed and rolled out for ground testing on March 15, 1952. The first flight was one month later on April 15. The YB-52 was the first B-52-type to actually fly.

[2] Congress found that the 2010 report on the Department of Defense Quadrennial Defense Review concluded that anti-access/area denial strategies and weapon systems "seek to deny outside countries the ability to project power into a region, thereby allowing aggression or other destabilizing actions to be conducted by the anti-access power. Without dominant capabilities to project power, the integrity of United States alliances and security partnerships could be called into question, reducing United States security and influence and increasing the possibility of conflict." P.L. 111-383, 111th Congress, 2nd session, 2011, Section 1238.

[3] For example, Lt. Gen. Christopher D. Miller, deputy chief of staff for Air Force strategic plans and programs noted, "The current fleet [of bombers] has been upgraded over the years with new weapons and electronic warfare systems, but it is increasingly at risk to modernizing air defenses." Quoted in John A. Tirpack's, "Time to Get Started," *Air Force Magazine*, February 2012, p. 31.

This report addresses potential congressional oversight and appropriations concerns for the sustainment and modernization of the U.S. Air Force's bomber force. It does not address Air Force efforts to develop and acquire the proposed LRS-B. Congressional interest in this subject stems from Congress's authority to approve, reject, or modify Air Force funding requests for bomber sustainment and modernization, as well as their oversight of the nation's long-range strike requirements and capabilities. In addition, sustainment, modernization, and size of the bomber force have been perennial legislative topics since the early 1990s. As the Air Force progresses through development and acquisition of the LRS-B and begins the gradual phase-out of 50-year-old bombers, it is anticipated that Congress will continue dealing with bomber sustainment and modernization legislation. Congress's decisions on appropriations for the bomber force could impact the nation's long-range strike capabilities and have additional consequences for the U.S. aerospace industry.

A key issue for Congress is whether to continue providing sustainment and modernization funding for the Air Force's B-52H, B-1B, and B-2A bombers, and if so, at what levels. Pertinent to the discussion is the potential for a shortfall in the nation's long-range strike capabilities if Congress or the Air Force chooses to minimize funding for sustainment and upgrades that would keep these weapon systems viable against A2/AD-equipped adversaries. Also, given Air Force plans to keep the B-52 and B-1 flying well beyond 2030, Congress may consider whether current bomber sustainment and modernization plans will meet the nation's long-range strike requirements until the LRS-B is operational. Additionally, Congress may also consider whether the planned 80-100 LRS-Bs will adequately replace the capabilities lost as the legacy bombers start retiring from service in the 2030s. Congress's oversight and decisions on these issues could also have implications for any potential future base realignment and closure (BRAC) decisions as well as impact the U.S. aircraft manufacturing industrial base. Ultimately, the priority the Air Force places on bomber sustainment and modernization, and any decisions considered by Congress, could have potential consequences for future national defense strategies and on U.S. long-range strike capabilities.

Background

United States' Military Strategy Shift: Do the Bombers' Capabilities Meet Strategic Requirements?

The Obama Administration's 2012 shift in national security and defense strategy towards the Asia-Pacific region has significant implications for America's legacy bomber force.[4] Stemming from the growing economic importance of the Asia-Pacific region, China's growing military capabilities and its increasing assertiveness of claims to disputed maritime territories, U.S. concerns with freedom of navigation and the ability to project power in the region, and the end of U.S. military operations in Iraq and Afghanistan, President Obama directed the Department of Defense (DOD) to raise the Asia-Pacific region's priority in U.S. military planning.[5] Many analysts agree this rebalance has placed renewed emphasis on U.S. naval forces due to the

---

[4] For in-depth analysis of the Obama Administration's rebalance towards Asia-Pacific, see CRS Report R42448, *Pivot to the Pacific? The Obama Administration's "Rebalancing" Toward Asia*, coordinated by Mark E. Manyin.

[5] For in-depth analysis of DOD's new strategic guidance, see CRS Report R42146, *Assessing the January 2012 Defense Strategic Guidance (DSG): In Brief*, by Catherine Dale and Pat Towell.

maritime character of the Pacific theater of operations. However, budgetary pressures and potential defense cuts may reduce long-term naval procurement plans and planned naval force levels in the Pacific region.[6] Consequently, just as B-17 and B-29 bombers demonstrated the value of long-range airpower projection in the Pacific Theater during World War II, the U.S. Air Force may be planning on the current fleet of B-52s, B-1s, and B-2s to provide an essential complement to U.S. naval forces in the vast geographical expanses of the Asia-Pacific.[7]

In addition to the Asia-Pacific, the Administration's new defense strategy also calls for retaining emphasis on the Middle East while ensuring U.S. defense commitments to European allies. This aspect of the new strategy may prove the most challenging from a resource perspective as the DOD is forced to implement automatic spending cuts laid out in the Budget Control Act (BCA) of 2011 (P.L. 112-25/S. 365 of August 2, 2011). The BCA necessitates $55 billion a year in defense cuts over the nine years from FY2013 to FY2021. Specifically for the bomber force, Air Force leaders have said that such cuts would result in an 18% reduction in both bomber flying hours and in bomber sustainment and modernization efforts, resulting in aircraft availability and mission capable rates falling below standards.[8] Some military analysts, consequently, are skeptical as to whether U.S. force levels will be sufficient to meet multiple, competing priorities in both the Asia-Pacific and the Middle East, all the while reassuring U.S. commitments in Europe.[9] However, some historical examples suggest the current bomber force is capable of balancing national security priorities among competing geographical regions.

Since 2003, B-52s, B-1s, and B-2s have maintained a continuous bomber presence in the Pacific with regularly scheduled rotations to Andersen Air Force Base, Guam, while simultaneously participating in continuous combat operations in the Middle East and Afghanistan. An example of this is the March 2003 deployment of B-52s and B-1s to Guam (in response to North Korean nuclear weapons activities) while additional B-52s, B-1s, and B-2s participated in the opening phases of Operation Iraqi Freedom and flew combat sorties in Afghanistan.[10] Essentially, this dual deployment of bombers to two geographical regions demonstrated the United States and the bomber force's ability to fight wars in the Middle East and Afghanistan while retaining the capability to respond to potential crises in the Asia-Pacific.

---

[6] For example, there is considerable concern that long-term Navy budgets will not sustain a Navy of 313 ships, as called for in recent plans. See, for instance, Jonathan Greenert, "Navy, 2025: Forward Warfighters," *U.S. Naval Institute Proceedings,* December 2011: 20 and 22.

[7] Ashton B. Carter, Deputy Secretary of Defense, "The U.S. Strategic Rebalance to Asia: A Defense Perspective" (speech, The Asia Society, New York, NY, August 1, 2012); and, Tom Vanden Brook, "B-1 bomber mission shifts from Afghanistan to China, Pacific," *USA Today online,* http://usatoday30.usatoday.com/news/military/story/2012-05-11/b-1-bomber-obama-new-strategy/56097706/1.

[8] Department of the U.S. Air Force, *Public Affairs Guidance: Sequestration-Final* (Washington, DC: USAF Public Affairs Office, February 7, 2013).

[9] For example, Dan Blumenthal, director of Asian Studies at the American Enterprise Institute, assesses that the current U.S. response to China's military modernization, manifested in the Obama Administration's rebalance to the Asia-Pacific and the U.S. military's operational concept called Air-Sea Battle (ASB), is inadequate in several respects. Primarily, Blumenthal argues that cuts to the defense budget will make it difficult to resource the Administration's "rebalance" and the military's ASB concept while continuing to address challenges that remain in the Middle East and Europe. Dan Blumenthal et al., *Strategic Asia 2012-13: China's Military Challenge* (Washington, DC: The National Bureau of Asian Research, 2012), chapter on: The U.S. Response to China's Military, p 309.

[10] Rebecca Grant, "Bomber Diplomacy," *Air Force Magazine,* December 2011, 32.

Potential Strategic Influence of Bombers on the Administration's Strategy Shift

The Administration's strategic guidance identifies three priorities for which the USAF bomber force could have significant strategic influence. These include reaffirming U.S. commitment to the security and prosperity of allies in the Asia-Pacific region; ensuring access to the global commons which facilitate world-wide economic opportunities and guarantee U.S. power projection capabilities; and ensuring a quick, military response capability to any hostilities from potential adversaries in the region.

According to former Secretary of State Hillary Clinton, the U.S. commitment to what she termed "forward-deployed" diplomacy would include the strengthening of bilateral security alliances with U.S. allies in the Asia-Pacific and necessitate the forging of a broad-based military presence.[11] Forward based bombers, whether deployed on a continuous basis or periodically as part of training exercises, could play a significant role in reaffirming U.S. commitments to allies in the Asia-Pacific region. Primarily through regular rotational deployments (such as the continuous bomber presence rotation at Andersen AFB, Guam) and participation in bilateral and multilateral training exercises, the visible presence of U.S. bombers abroad could potentially reinforce the U.S. commitment to deterrence (conventional and nuclear) against any potential adversary in the region and could provide an economical and effective way to increase U.S. influence there.[12]

Freedom of navigation and access to the South China Sea is considered by many analysts vital to the economy of every nation in North America and East Asia. More than half of the world's shipping passes through the South China Sea every year (approximately 70,000 ships carrying $5.3 trillion worth of goods). Of that, $1.2 trillion worth is trade that directly affects the United States.[13] In addition, over 80% of crude oil supplies to Japan, South Korea, and Taiwan flow through the South China Sea—making these countries especially dependent on South China Sea shipping routes.[14] Any attempt to restrict universal access to this maritime common could impact the security, political stability, and economic prosperity of the United States and its allies in the region and potentially inhibit U.S. power projection capabilities by restricting the U.S. Navy's ability to patrol and operate in the South China Sea and the Malacca Straits. Long-range bombers, conducting maritime reconnaissance and capable of anti-shipping operations, could actively and passively maintain situational awareness of the vast Asia-Pacific maritime region and possibly keep in check any potential adversary looking to threaten the United States and its allies' access to the Asia-Pacific's commons.

---

[11] Hillary Clinton, "America's Pacific Century," *Foreign Policy*, November 2011, http://www.foreignpolicy.com/articles/2011/10/11/americas_pacific_century

[12] United States Pacific Command participates in multiple exercises and other engagement activities throughout the Asia-Pacific region which the bomber force has or could take part in. These bilateral and multilateral exercises include TALISMAN SABER, a biennial Australia/United States bilateral exercise; COBRA GOLD, a joint/combined exercise with Thailand; BALIKATAN, a joint exercise with the Republic of the Philippines; KEEN SWORD/KEEN EDGE, a joint/bilateral exercise with Japan; and, RIM OF THE PACIFIC, a biennial large-scale multinational power projection and sea control exercise.

[13] Bonnie S. Glaser, Senior Fellow, Center for Strategic and International Studies, "Armed Clash in the South China Sea: Contingency Planning Memorandum No. 14," http://www.cfr.org/east-asia/armed-clash-south-china-sea/p27883, February 14, 2013.

[14] Office of the Secretary of Defense, "Annual Report to Congress-Military Power of the People's Republic of China 2008," p 11, http://www.defense.gov/pubs/pdfs/China_Military_Report_08.pdf.

Finally, the legacy bomber force is one option than can produce a quick, military response to hostile actions taken by potential adversaries in the region. Unconstrained by the need for a forward operating location within theater, the capability of bombers to reach anywhere in the Asia-Pacific, in a relatively short period of time and with a wide array of weapons, could provide national leaders a viable option for responding to encroachments on U.S. interests in the region and for honoring defense and security commitments to U.S. allies.

Bomber Expectations: Employment in DOD's Strategic Guidance

Bomber Contribution to Critical Missions

The Administration's new strategic guidance emphasizes the military's need to recalibrate its capabilities and make selective investments to succeed in a number of missions critical to achieving national security objectives.[15] Any argument for or against any level of funding for bomber modernization could include an assessment and cost/benefit analysis of those upgrades and their contribution to accomplishing the expected missions of U.S. forces as defined in the DOD's strategic guidance, *Sustaining U.S. Global Leadership: Priorities for 21st Century Defense*. These missions include the following:[16]

- Counter terrorism and irregular warfare;
- deter and defeat aggression;
- project power despite anti-access/area denial challenges;
- counter weapons of mass destruction;
- operate effectively in cyberspace and space;
- maintain a safe, secure, and effective nuclear deterrent;
- provide a stabilizing presence; and,
- conduct stability and counterinsurgency operations.

---

[15] Department of Defense, *Sustaining U.S. Global Leadership: Priorities for 21st Century Defense,* January 2012 (Washington, DC), 4-6.

[16] Ibid.

All three of the nation's bombers have made, and are expected to continue making, significant contributions to all of the critical missions set forth in DOD's strategic guidance. Looking as far back as 1962 (coinciding with the last B-52 delivery), numerous examples describe one or more of the current bombers accomplishing these missions (see **Table 1**). However, with the rising prevalence of 21st century A2/AD capabilities in several potential adversary countries, even the U.S. Air Force assesses that modern threat capabilities are outpacing the 20th century capabilities and abilities of the B-52, B-1 and, in some circumstances, even the B-2, to accomplish these missions.[17] Without funding for critical modernization and sustainment efforts, all three bombers run the risk of becoming ineffective in the face of A2/AD equipped adversaries.[18]

---

[17] The U.S. Air Force acknowledges in its 2012 Posture Statement that, "as A2/AD capabilities proliferate, our [U.S. Air Force] fourth-generation fighter and legacy bomber capability to penetrate contested airspace is increasingly challenged" and "Procuring a new penetrating bomber is critical to maintaining our [U.S. Air Force] long-range strike capability in the face of evolving A2/AD environments." Department of the Air Force, *United States Air Force Posture Statement*, Washington, DC, 2012, 15-16.

[18] Anti-Access/Area Denial (A2/AD) capabilities are meant to frustrate the U.S.' ability to project substantial military capability over considerable strategic and operational distances. A2 capabilities are designed to exclude U.S. forces from a foreign theater or deny effective use and transit of the global commons such as air, maritime, space and cyberspace. AD capabilities are designed to complicate U.S. force's ability to establish a presence and effectively operate in, over, or in range of an adversary's territory or interests. Twenty-first century AD capabilities can attack U.S. vulnerabilities in all five key operating domains—air, sea, land, space, and cyberspace.

Table 1. Historical Examples of Missions Accomplished by Bombers

(1962-Present)

Conflict/Crisis	Bomber	Counter Terror/Irreg Warfare	Deter/Defeat Aggression	Power Projection	Counter WMD	Operate in Cyberspace	Nuclear Deterrent	Stabilizing Presence	Stability/ COIN Operations
Cold War 1947-1991	B-52, B-1		X	X	X		X	X	
Cuban Missile Crisis 1962	B-52			X			X	X	
Vietnam War 1959-1975	B-52	X	X						X
Desert Storm 1991	B-52		X	X	X				
Desert Fox 1998	B-52, B-1		X	X	X				
Allied Force 1999	B-52, B-1, B-2		X	X		X			
Afghanistan 2001-present	B-52, B-1, B-2	X	X	X		X			X
Iraq 2003-2011	B-52, B-1, B-2	X	X	X	X	X	X		X

Source: Prepared by CRS based on analysis of the historical use of bombers by the United States Air Force, 1947 to 2013.

Forward Deployed Diplomacy: Continuous Bomber Presence and Worldwide Power Projection

With the conclusion of U.S. military involvement in Iraq and U.S. forces drawing down in Afghanistan, DOD has announced it intends to shift military capacity from the Middle East to the Asia-Pacific region as part of the Obama Administration's rebalancing strategy. On multiple occasions, Deputy Secretary of Defense Ashton Carter has stated DOD's intent to begin rotating B-1 bombers (which have been the only bomber participating in Operation Enduring Freedom since May 2006) into the Asia-Pacific region to augment B-52s already on continuous rotation there.[19] This continuous rotation—referred to by the DOD as the Continuous Bomber Presence (CBP)—is based at Andersen Air Force Base, Guam, and represents a major investment in ensuring U.S. security commitments in the Pacific.

Capable of reaching anywhere in the U.S. Pacific Command's (USPACOM's) area of responsibility with weapons ranging from conventional to nuclear-tipped cruise missiles, the CBP is one way of reassuring allies of the U.S. commitment to their defense and deterring potential adversaries in the region, including possibly China. The CBP can potentially send the signal that no naval vessel can patrol the South China Sea and Pacific without coming under the reach of land-based bombers. According to former Pacific Air Forces commander General Gary L. North, "Chinese military writings talk a lot about how to extend their power to the second island chain … the 1,800 mile [factor], which would enable them to prevent other nations' ability to have freedom of movement at that great range."[20] Invoking the lessons learned from the Pacific Theater of World War II, the CBP, and long-range airpower projection in general, could be seen as an essential complement in dealing with potential adversary naval forces.

Air Force Global Strike Command recently announced B-2s will begin regular worldwide training deployments to each of the regional U.S. combatant commands' areas of responsibility starting in 2013.[21] According to 8th Air Force Commander Major General Stephen Wilson, B-2s will rotate to forward operating locations all over the world in small numbers for a few weeks at a time, a set number of times a year beginning with a short Pacific deployment in 2013.[22] The plan calls for B-2 deployments to all the geographic combatant commands including those in Central and South America, Southwest Asia, and Europe in addition to the Asia-Pacific.[23] These worldwide training deployments are an exercise in power projection and meant to demonstrate U.S. commitments to allies in multiple regions of the world while providing a visible deterrent to any potential U.S. adversary.

Military analysts point out that engaging in this type of "forward deployed diplomacy" with the bomber force has the potential to influence the Asia-Pacific region beyond the near-term concern

---

[19] Ashton B. Carter, Deputy Secretary of Defense, "The U.S. Strategic Rebalance to Asia: A Defense Perspective" (speech, The Asia Society, New York, NY, August 1, 2012) and (address, remarks on China's Military Challenge, Woodrow Wilson Center, Washington, DC, October 3, 2012).

[20] Statement of General Gary L. North, former Pacific Air Forces Commander, in Rebecca Grant's, "Bomber Diplomacy," *Air Force Magazine*, December 2011, 31.

[21] Arie Church, "Spirit World Tour, Coming to a Theater Near You." *Air Force Magazine.com*, November 9, 2012, http://www.airforce-magazine.com/Pages/HomePage.aspx.

[22] Ibid.

[23] Ibid.

of a rising China. Give the efforts by numerous Asian-Pacific states seeking to increase their diplomatic, economic, and strategic influence in the region, the potential exists for a number of regional players to acquire advanced military capabilities that could influence long-term U.S. interests and/or threaten U.S. access to the region in the future. For example, North Korea's continuing efforts to develop an intercontinental ballistic missile capability, along with its nuclear weapons program, represent a potential direct threat to the United States and threaten to undermine regional security. South Korea, in an effort to offset its strategic vulnerabilities, has undergone a vigorous procurement and acquisition of state-of-the-art weaponry and has invested over $25 billion a year since 2006 on indigenous research and development programs for its local defense industries.[24] Japan, after years of watching its international influence eroded by a slow-motion economic decline, is attempting to raise its relevance in the region by offering military aid to regional neighbors and by stepping up training and engagement activities by its own armed forces in an effort to build regional alliances and shore up other countries' defenses.[25] India, who until the recent global economic downturn possessed the second-fastest-growing economy in the world, became the largest weapons importer in the world in March 2011. It is anticipated that India will spend up to $80 billion on military modernization by 2015, and it is considered by many analysts to be on the verge of attaining military superpower status.[26] Indonesia, supported by its military leadership and a $16.7 billion budget, is moving forward with a three-year plan to strengthen and modernize its military arsenal to include $2.5 billion for 10 light frigates, $2 billion for four submarines, and $6 billion for the addition of Russian Sukhoi and U.S. F-16 fighters.[27] Taiwan, who is falling rapidly behind the unprecedented Chinese military buildup over the past decade, conducted tests of a new "carrier killer" anti-ship missile in late 2012. Thought to be an advanced version of the Hsiung Feng III anti-ship missile, such a weapon could pose a significant challenge to any naval vessel operating in the Taiwan Straits if developed in sufficient numbers.[28] The point being, there is no doubt that with the enormous amount of economic, military, and political power concentrated in the Asia-Pacific region, the proliferation of A2/AD weapon systems could impact the future of U.S. influence and capacity in the region, regardless of who possesses such capabilities.

CBP rotations and regular B-2 deployments stand to play a long-term role in the United States' ability to influence and project military power in the Asia-Pacific, provided bomber sustainment and modernization efforts keep pace with current and evolving A2/AD military capabilities that are becoming prevalent in the region. However, with such emphasis being placed on military

---

[24] Georgetown Journal of International Affairs, *South Korea's Unsustainable Military Build-Up*, January 28, 2013, http://journal.georgetown.edu/2013/01/28/south-koreas-unsustainable-military-build-up-by-jeong-lee/.

[25] Martin Fackler, *Japan Is Flexing Its Military Muscle to Counter a Rising China* (*The New York Times*, November 26, 2012), http://www.nytimes.com/2012/11/27/world/asia/japan-expands-its-regional-military-role html?pagewanted=all

[26] The Stockholm International Peace Research Institute (SIPRI) reported in March 2011 that India is now the largest weapons importer in the world, receiving 9% of the volume of international arms transfers during the period 2006 to 2010. Stockholm International Peace Research Institute, *India world's largest arms importer according to new SIPRI data on international arms transfers*, March 14, 2011, http://www.sipri.org/media/pressreleases/2011/armstransfers, and, Center for Strategic & International Studies, Current Issues No. 24: India's Defense Spending and Military Modernization (3/29/2011), http://csis.org/files/publication/110329_DIIG_Current_Issues_24_Indian_Defense_Spending.pdf.

[27] Michael Johnson, *Indonesian Military Plans to Spend $16.7 Billion Through 2015*, Asia Pacific Defense Forum, October 22, 2012, http://apdforum.com/en_GB/article/rmiap/articles/online/features/2012/10/22/indonesia-military-spends

[28] Harry Kazianis, *To Counter China's Military Build-up, Taiwan Must Go Asymmetric*, World Politics Review, November 29, 2012, http://www.worldpoliticsreview.com/articles/12529/to-counter-chinas-military-build-up-taiwan-must-go-asymmetric.

modernization by many of the major states in the region, it is hard to predict what the strategic and military landscape of the Asia-Pacific will look like in 20 or 30 years. Such a time frame could potentially see the B-52, B-1, and B-2 still in service; if so, they will be expected to be effective weapon systems if employed.

Meeting the Anti-Access/Area Denial (A2/AD) Challenge

A major challenge in meeting the goals of the Administration's new strategy is the rising prevalence of 21st century anti-access/area denial (A2/AD) threats. Anti-access refers to those adversary actions and capabilities, usually employed from long ranges, designed to prevent an opposing force entry to an operational area by restricting its access to the global commons (sea, air, space, and cyberspace). Area denial refers to those adversary actions and capabilities, usually of shorter range, designed not to keep an opposing force out, but to limit its freedom of action within an operational area.[29] Although not a new concept, A2/AD is a rising concern due to the proliferation of technology that places precise, long-range weapons in the hands of potential foes. Such weapons include ballistic and cruise missiles, integrated air defense systems, anti-ship missiles, submarines, guided rockets, missiles and artillery, 4th- and 5th-generation combat aircraft, and space and cyber warfare capabilities. Many of these A2/AD threats are specifically designed to challenge the U.S. military's power projection capabilities and potentially threaten U.S. access to key areas of strategic interest both in the Asia-Pacific and the Middle East.

The U.S. military addresses the A2/AD challenge in its *Joint Operational Access Concept* (JOAC). Although not enemy- or region-specific, JOAC describes how joint forces will operate in response to the emerging A2/AD threat. Its central idea hinges on the joint forces' ability to leverage cross-domain synergy—the complementary employment of military capabilities across the sea, air, land, space, and cyberspace domains that enhances the effectiveness of military operations and compensates for any known weaknesses in U.S. capabilities.[30] The Air Force and Navy have embraced cross-domain synergy and have codified their approach to the A2/AD challenge in their *Air-Sea Battle Concept* (ASBC). ASBC seeks to achieve interoperability between air and naval forces that can execute networked, integrated attacks, in-depth, to disrupt, destroy, and defeat an adversary's A2/AD capabilities.[31] ASBC and the idea of cross-domain synergy as an answer to the A2/AD challenge have very real implications for the modernization and operational employment of the bomber force; primarily, modernization and sustainment efforts should equip the bomber force with the capabilities necessary to operate in the extreme-, high-, and low-risk denied regions of the 21st century A2/AD environment.

---

[29] Department of Defense, *"Joint Operational Access Concept (JOAC),"* Version 1.0, November 22, 2011, p. i.

[30] Ibid., p. ii.

[31] General Norton A. Schwartz, USAF and Admiral Jonathan W. Greenert, USN, *"Air-Sea Battle: Promoting Stability in an Era of Uncertainty,"* (The American Interest, February 20, 2012), http://www.the-american-interest.com/article.cfm?piece=1212. Stated another way, ASBC seek to integrate and take advantage of the differing capabilities afforded by a diverse joint force (air, ground and naval forces), armed with the latest in resilient communications (networked), in order to target and strike (integrated attack) multiple enemy targets and systems (attack-in-depth) that will reduce or eliminate an enemy's A2/AD capability thus enabling the U.S. military to operate freely in what was previously, a highly defended area.

Figure 1. Joint Operational Access and Air-Sea Battle Concept

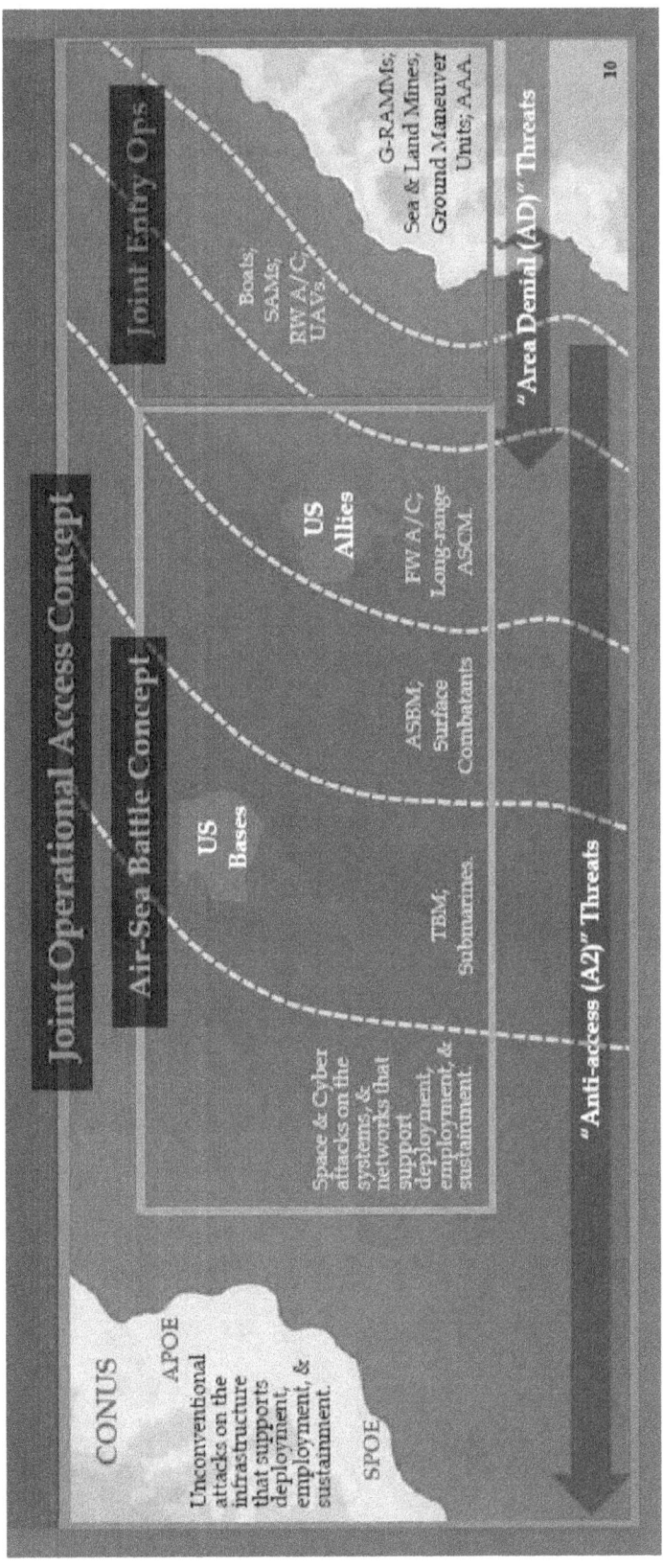

Source: Pentagon briefing, Mr. William Dries, Air Force Air-Sea Battle Team, subject: Air-Sea Battle: A Primer (lecture, USAF Fellowship Orientation, Pentagon), July 31, 2012.

Bomber Employment in an A2/AD Environment

One of the objectives of an A2/AD adversary is to establish what the military terms extreme-risk geographic zones in order to deny any advantage to U.S. forces operating in them. In extreme-risk zones, only the most capable, low-signature (stealthy) forces maintain the ability to survive and operate effectively using self-defense systems, maneuver and, in some cases, additional support to do so.[32] Due to its stealth and self-defense capabilities, the B-2 is the most capable bomber able to operate in the extreme-risk zone.

In high-risk zones, the majority of U.S. high-signature (non-stealthy) forces require significant defense support. For the bombers, this means their defensive countermeasures and maneuvers will be effective if assisted by mutually supporting forces, but on their own, they may be operationally ineffective and limited.[33] The U.S. bombers most capable of operating in the high-risk zone are the B-2 (because of its stealth and self-defense capabilities) and the B-1 given its speed, maneuverability, low-altitude flying capability, and electronic self-defense capabilities.

In the low-risk zone—usually found at extended ranges from the adversary's borders—all U.S. forces can generally operate freely, although the adversary can potentially still pose a threat. The B-1 and B-52 are quite capable of operating in low-risk zones and would most likely employ their arsenal of long-range, standoff cruise missiles (the B-2 does not carry long-range stand-off cruise missiles). In the overall Air-Sea Battle Concept, higher-signature forces—such as the B-1 and B-52—would be teamed with low-signature forces as required—such as the stealthy F-22 fighter—in order to enhance the effectiveness and compensate for the vulnerabilities of each platform. Nevertheless, the challenge is that the Air Force's legacy bombers could have increasing difficulty operating in A2/AD environments without more modern systems and weapons capabilities.

---

[32] Mr. William Dries, Air Force Air-Sea Battle Team, "Air-Sea Battle: A Primer," (lecture, USAF Fellowship Orientation, Pentagon), July 31, 2012.

[33] Ibid.

Figure 2. Legacy Bomber Employment in an A2/AD Operating Environment

Source: Pentagon briefing, Mr. William Dries, Air Force Air-Sea Battle Team, subject: Air-Sea Battle: A Primer (lecture, USAF Fellowship Orientation, Pentagon) July 31, 2012.

Nuclear Deterrent Operations

Under DOD's strategic guidance, maintaining a safe, secure, and effective nuclear deterrent remains a primary mission for U.S. Armed Forces. Its guidance is coherent with and builds on the 2010 *Quadrennial Defense Review* (QDR) which states, "Until such time as the Administration's goal of a world free of nuclear weapons is achieved, nuclear capabilities will be maintained as a core mission of the Department of Defense."[34] Relevant to the bomber force, the 2010 *Nuclear Posture Review* (NPR) reaffirmed the enduring contributions and viability of the nuclear strike capabilities of the B-52 and the B-2 in accomplishing the nuclear deterrent mission (the B-1 is no longer nuclear capable).[35]

Proponents argue three principal reasons for retaining and modernizing nuclear-capable, or, more accurately, dual-capable B-52 and B-2 bombers. First, an air-delivered nuclear capability provides a rapid and direct hedge against technical challenges with the other legs of the nuclear triad as well as geopolitical uncertainties.[36]

Second, nuclear-capable bombers are important to extended deterrence of potential attacks on U.S. allies and partners. Unlike intercontinental ballistic missiles (ICBMs) and submarine launched ballistic missiles (SLBMs), heavy bombers can be visibly forward deployed, thereby signaling U.S. resolve and commitment in a crisis.

Finally, not only is the LRS-B not anticipated to start flight testing until the mid-2020s, it is also yet to be determined if it will initially be nuclear capable once it does. Former Chief of Staff of the Air Force General Norton Schwartz testified before Congress in November 2011 that the new LRS-B will be built with nuclear capability but will operate as a conventional strike aircraft initially. He stressed that although the aircraft will be designed and built with all the hardware for both nuclear and conventional missions from the outset, "Deferring the new aircraft's nuclear certification until the B-52 and B-2 start to retire would help the service manage costs."[37] However, in response to General Schwartz's testimony, language in the 2013 Defense Authorization Act (P.L. 112-239) stipulates the next-generation LRS-B will be "capable of carrying strategic nuclear weapons as of the date on which such aircraft achieves initial operating capability" and will be "certified to use such weapons by not later than two years after such date." If the nation wishes to maintain an air-delivered nuclear capability, as stated in the 2010 QDR and NPR, it is unclear whether the B-52 and B-2 will be the only air-delivery option in the U.S. nuclear arsenal until the 2030s or whether the LRS-B can be expected to start filling that role in the late 2020s.

---

[34] Department of Defense, *Quadrennial Defense Review Report* (Washington, DC: February 2010), vi.

[35] Department of Defense, *Nuclear Posture Review Report* (Washington, DC: April 2010), 24.

[36] The U.S. nuclear triad includes the long-range nuclear-capable bomber force (76, B-52s and 20, B-2s), 450 Minuteman III intercontinental ballistic missiles (ICBM), and 14 Ohio Class submarines capable of launching 24 Trident II submarine launched ballistic missiles (SLBM) each. Unlike ICBMs and submarine—which are designed to remain hidden from view of an adversary—the bomber fleet offers a visible way of conveying U.S. resolve. For example, the president could order the nation's B-52s and B-2s on alert, put them in the air, and/or deploy them to forward bases thus providing a visible sign of U.S. resolve with the intent of de-escalating tensions. Many analysts agree that the visible presence of bombers provides the U.S. an effective tool for overtly demonstrating resolve.

[37] David Majumdar, "Schwartz: New Bomber Not Nuke-Capable at First," *Air Force Times Online*, November 2, 2011, http://www.airforcetimes.com/news/2011/11/dn-air-force-new-bomber-nuclear-capable-11-211/.

New Strategic Arms Reduction Treaty: Impact on Bombers

In accordance with the New Strategic Arms Reduction Treaty (NST) signed in April 2010, the United States and Russia plan on reducing and limiting ICBMs and ICBM launchers, SLBMs and SLBM launchers, heavy bombers, ICBM warheads, SLBM warheads, and heavy bomber nuclear armaments. Seven years after entry into force of the treaty and thereafter, the aggregate numbers, as counted in accordance with Article II section one of the treaty, will not exceed 700 for deployed ICBMs, deployed SLBMs, and deployed heavy bombers. Also, the total numbers will not exceed 800 for deployed and non-deployed ICBM launchers, deployed and non-deployed SLBM launchers, and deployed and non-deployed heavy bombers.[38] The United States retains the right to determine for itself the composition and structure of its strategic offensive arms.[39]

Consequently, the February 2011 entry-into-force of the New START drives the United States to convert a number of nuclear-capable B-52 bombers to a conventional-only role. Although a final force structure decision has not been made to reflect the requirements of New START, Air Force Global Strike Command (AFGSC) recommended a preferred course of action in the FY13 Program Objective Memorandum (POM) and funded through the future years defense program (FYDP).[40] The New START drives no change to the configuration of B-2 force numbers.

In her statement before the Senate Foreign Relations Committee, Ms. Madelyn Creedon, Assistant Secretary of Defense for Global Strategic Affairs, provided testimony on the need for bomber sustainment and modernization in the context of implementing the New Start Treaty:

> The United States will maintain two nuclear capable B-52H strategic bomber wings and one B-2A wing. Both bombers, however, are aging and sustainment and modernization funding will have to be provided to ensure they remain operationally effective through the remainder of their service lives. Funding has been allocated to upgrade these platforms; for example, to provide the B-2A with survivable communications, a more modern flight control system, and a new radar. The B-52 will also need various upgrades including for its bomb bay and survivable communications. These modernization and sustainment programs are needed to maintain the effectiveness of the current bomber force until the introduction of a new long-range bomber.[41]

Existing U.S. Bomber Force

The Air Force's existing bomber fleet includes 76 B-52H bombers, 63 supersonic B-1B bombers, and 20 B-2 stealth bombers. **Table 2** summarizes the three types of aircraft. Additional information on the existing bomber force is presented in **Appendix A**.

---

[38] For in-depth analysis of the New START Treaty, see CRS Report R41219, *The New START Treaty: Central Limits and Key Provisions*, by Amy F. Woolf.

[39] *Treaty Between the United States of America and the Russian Federation on Measures for the Further Reduction and Limitation of Strategic Offensive Arms*, April 8, 2010.

[40] Air Force Global Strike Command, *B-52 Bomber Master Plan*, June 2012, p 19.

[41] Testimony of Madelyn Creedon, Assistant Secretary of Defense for Global Strategic Affairs, in Senate, *Hearings before the Senate Foreign Relations Committee*, 112th Congress, 2nd Session., June 21, 2012.

Table 2. Current U.S. Air Force Bomber Force

	B-52H	B-1B	B-2
Number in inventory	76	63[a]	20
Number combat ready	44	36	16
First flight	1954	1984	1988
Last delivery	1962	1988	1997
Unrefueled range	8,800	7,455	6,000+
Payload	70,000	75,000	40,000+
Crew	5	4	2
Max speed	Mach .86	Mach 1.2 (sea level)	High Subsonic

Source: Prepared by CRS based on *Air Force Almanac*, May 2012 and U.S. Air Force B-52, B-1, and B-2 Fact Sheets.

a. Three B-1s were retired as requested by the U.S. Air Force in their 2012 budget request and in accordance with direction put forth in the 2012 National Defense Authorization Act (P.L. 112-81).

B-52H Stratofortress[42]

Figure 3. B-52H Stratofortress

Source: U.S. Air Force official website, B-52 Stratofortress Factsheet (http://www.af.mil/information/factsheets/).

The B-52 is currently the USAF's only nuclear bomber capable of employing long-range standoff weapons. It serves both as a nuclear and conventional bomber. It first entered operational service on June 29, 1955. The B-52's original service life expectancy was approximately 5,000 hours or approximately 20 years depending on severity of the flying environment. Of the 744 various

---

[42] Information in this section is taken from Air Force Global Strike Command's, *B-52 Bomber Master Plan*, June 2012, *Air Force Almanac*, May 2012, and U.S. Air Force B-52 Fact Sheet, December 4, 2012, http://www.af mil/information/factsheets/factsheet.asp?id=83.

model B-52s built, 76 B-52H models remain in service today. The B-52H first entered service on May 9, 1961, with operational aircraft currently stationed at Barksdale AFB, Louisiana, and Minot AFB, North Dakota. The B-52's life expectancy has been extended beyond original expectations through numerous modernization efforts. It is now projected to be sustainable into 2040 based on projected average flying hours and severity of the flying environment.

The B-52H program's challenge is to continue sustainment activities and maintain combat effectiveness against the nation's adversaries until the platform is retired, and to approach modernization efforts effectively by recognizing capability gaps, prioritizing valid requirements, and investing in material solutions that meet platform and war fighter needs. As plans for sustainment, modernization, and recapitalization move forward, some argue the B-52 enterprise should be prepared to make required programmatic and operational adjustments in step with changes in platform mission taskings and operational plans. The B-52's strengths lie in its diverse capabilities, precision, large payload, and long range; however, if these capabilities remain static, mission effectiveness is likely to erode in the face of 21st century A2/AD threats.

Current B-52 Sustainment and Modernization Efforts[43]

The following is a list of B-52 sustainment and modernization initiatives in the program of record (POR) that are either just being completed or are currently in progress. Additional information on each effort, as well as information on short-term and long-term sustainment and modernization efforts, can be found in the B-52's Master Plan summarized in **Appendix B**.

- Combat network communications technology (CONECT)

- Military-standard-1760 modernization

- B-52 trainer upgrades

- Arms control activities under the New START

- Mode S/5 identification friend or foe (IFF)

- Low cost modifications

- B-52 anti-skid replacement

- B-52 modernization research development test and evaluation efforts

- 1760 internal weapons bay upgrade (IWBU)

Table 3 is the FY2013 budget submission for B-52 procurement and B-52 research, development, test, and evaluation programs derived from Air Force budget justification books. It summarizes prior-year and estimated future-year expenditures for B-52 sustainment and modernization programs.

---

[43] Information for current B-52 sustainment and modernization efforts derived from justification books for Air Force procurement accounts and Air Force research, development test and evaluation accounts for FY2013 and prior years.

Table 3. Current B-52 Sustainment and Modernization Efforts
(in millions of dollars)

Procurement Items	Total Cost All Prior Yrs	Total Cost FY2011	Total Cost FY2012	Total Cost FY2013	Total Cost FY2014	Total Cost FY2015	Total Cost FY2016	Total Cost FY2017	Cost To Complete	Total Cost
B-52 CONECT	8.971	6.416	82.531	0.000	0.000	17.519	25.604	23.298	2.543	166.882
MIL-STD-1760	0.000	11.541	0.000	3.238	30.983	6.690	0.000	0.000	0.000	52.452
B-52 Trainers	0.000	2.180	1.656	1.482	1.836	2.375	2.431	2.472	0.000	14.432
B-52 Structures	0.000	0.000	0.100	0.000	0.000	0.000	0.000	0.000	0.000	0.100
System Effectiveness and Evolutionary Requirements	0.000	0.000	0.100	0.000	0.000	0.000	0.000	0.000	0.000	0.100
Arms Control Activities	0.000	0.000	0.000	0.000	0.500	0.203	0.102	0.203	0.000	1.008
Mode S/5 IFF	0.000	0.000	8.725	0.000	9.590	12.357	2.557	0.000	0.000	33.229
Low Cost Mods	1.646	0.821	0.785	0.435	0.019	0.604	0.453	0.460	0.000	5.223
B-52 Anti-Skid Replacement	0.000	0.000	0.000	4.626	6.737	6.011	0.915	0.930	0.000	19.219

RDT&E Items	Total Cost FY2011	Total Cost FY2012	Total Cost FY2013	Total Cost FY2014	Total Cost FY2015	Total Cost FY2016	Total Cost FY2017	Cost To Complete	Total Cost
Misc. B-52 Modernization RDT&E Efforts	129.864	93.808	0.065					Continuing	Continuing
1760 Internal Wpns Bay Upgrade			16.490	11.373	5.653	3.901		Continuing	Continuing
Mode S/5 IFF			1.202					Continuing	Continuing
B-52 CONECT			34.700	29.800				Continuing	Continuing
B-52 Anti-Skid			0.751					Continuing	Continuing

Source: Prepared by CRS based on justification books for Air Force procurement accounts and Air Force research, development, test, and evaluation accounts for FY2013 and prior years.

B-1B Lancer[44]

Figure 4. B-1B Lancer

Source: U.S. Air Force official website, B-1B Lancer Factsheet (http://www.af.mil/information/factsheets/).

The B-1B Lancer was developed by Rockwell International, now Boeing Defense and Space Group, and became operational in 1986. The B-1B was originally designed to serve as a low-altitude Cold War supersonic bomber. Its low radar cross-section, variable-geometry wings, avionics, and afterburning engines made it less vulnerable than the B-52 to enemy surface-to-air missiles and fighter aircraft. However, following the end of the Cold War, the Air Force ended the B-1's nuclear mission in 1992 and began the aircraft's transition to conventional-only weapons capability. The Conventional Mission Upgrade Program (CMUP) transformed the B-1B into a conventional-only bomber capable of employing the latest in conventional weapons to include Global Positioning System (GPS)-guided Joint Directed Attack Munitions (JDAM) and long-range standoff Joint Air-to-Surface Stand-off Missiles (JASSM). The B-1B has the largest internal payload of any current bomber. However, many of the systems on the B-1 are original equipment and suffer from diminishing manufacturing sources and material shortfalls that impact reliability, availability, and maintainability.

One hundred B-1Bs were initially built, of which 63 remain in service. The fleet operates from Dyess AFB, Texas (35 aircraft), and Ellsworth AFB, South Dakota (28 aircraft). It possesses diverse capabilities: large precision payload, range, speed, and endurance; however, if these capabilities remain static, mission effectiveness may erode in the face of 21st century A2/AD threats. The B-1B is expected to be in service until 2040.

---

[44] Information in this section taken from Air Combat Command's, *B-1 Strategic Action and Investment Plan (SAIP)*, May 10, 2012; CRS Report RL34406, *Air Force Next-Generation Bomber: Background and Issues for Congress*, by Jeremiah Gertler; *Air Force Almanac, May 2012*; and U.S. Air Force B-1 Fact Sheet, May 21, 2012, http://www.af.mil/information/factsheets/factsheet.asp?fsID=81.

Current B-1 Sustainment and Modernization Efforts[45]

The following is a list of B-1 sustainment and modernization initiatives currently in the program of record (POR) that are either just completing or are currently in progress. Additional information on each effort, as well as information on short-term and long-term sustainment and modernization efforts, can be found in the B-1's Strategic Action and Investment Plan (SAIP) summarized in **Appendix C**.

- Fully integrated data link
- Simulator digital control loading
- Central integrated test system
- Inertial navigation system replacement
- Radar improvement upgrade
- Visual situation display upgrade
- Self-contained attitude indicator
- Gyro stabilization system replacement (GSSR)
- B-1 training support
- Digital communications
- B-1 Link 16 cryptographic materials
- Laptop controlled targeting pod
- Low cost mods
- Miscellaneous B-1 modernization research, development, test, and evaluation efforts

Table 4 is the FY2013 budget submission for B-1 procurement and B-1 research, development, test ,and evaluation programs derived from Air Force budget justification books. It summarizes prior-year and estimated future-year expenditures for B-1 sustainment and modernization programs.

---

[45] Information for current B-1B sustainment and modernization efforts derived from justification books for Air Force procurement accounts and Air Force research, development, test, and evaluation accounts for FY2013 and prior years.

Table 4. Current B-1 Sustainment and Modernization Efforts

(in millions of dollars)

Procurement Items	Total Cost FY2011	Total Cost FY2012	Total Cost FY2013	Total Cost FY2014	Total Cost FY2015	Total Cost FY2016	Total Cost FY2017	Cost To Complete	Total Cost
Fully Integrated Data Link	52.956	58.874	57.073	48.234	37.241	50.017	51.539	97.943	453.877
Simulator Digital Control Loading	0.000	0.000	2.700	2.800	2.937	0.000	0.000	0.000	8.437
CITS Upgrade	20.933	15.683	17.549	17.834	13.895	16.914	17.054	50.052	169.914
Inertial Navigation System	17.000	35.999	21.447	19.192	2.231	0.000	0.000	0.000	95.869
Radar Improvement Upgrade	59.126	44.302	10.512	1.692	2.586	0.242	0.000	0.000	175.091
Vertical Situation Displays	27.086	33.872	34.429	36.322	29.932	41.621	42.406	107.234	352.902
Self-Contained Attitude Indicator	0.000	0.000	0.000	1.700	2.025	1.835	1.730	1.367	8.657
Gyro Stabilization System	8.735	4.476	4.526	4.153	0.000	0.000	0.000	0.000	64.721
B-1 Training Supt	0.394	0.301	0.269	0.333	0.431	0.442	0.450	0.000	3.005
Digital Comms	5.257	1.600	0.000	0.000	0.000	0.000	0.000	0.000	34.348
B-1 Link 16 Crypto	0.000	0.000	0.000	0.221	0.325	0.089	0.000	0.000	0.635
Laptop Controlled Targeting Pod	4.882	1.000	0.000	0.000	0.000	0.000	0.000	0.000	67.658
Low Cost Mods	1.114	1.900	1.251	0.000	0.000	0.000	0.000	0.000	4.277

RDT&E Items	Total Cost FY2011	Total Cost FY2012	Total Cost FY2013	Total Cost FY2014	Total Cost FY2015	Total Cost FY2016	Total Cost FY2017	Cost To Complete	Total Cost
Misc. B-1 Modernization RDT&E Efforts	33.063	33.011	16.265	19.589	11.453	0.087		Continuing	Continuing

Source: Prepared by CRS based on justification books for Air Force procurement accounts and Air Force research, development test and evaluation accounts for FY2013 and prior years.

B-2A Spirit[46]

Figure 5. B-2A Spirit

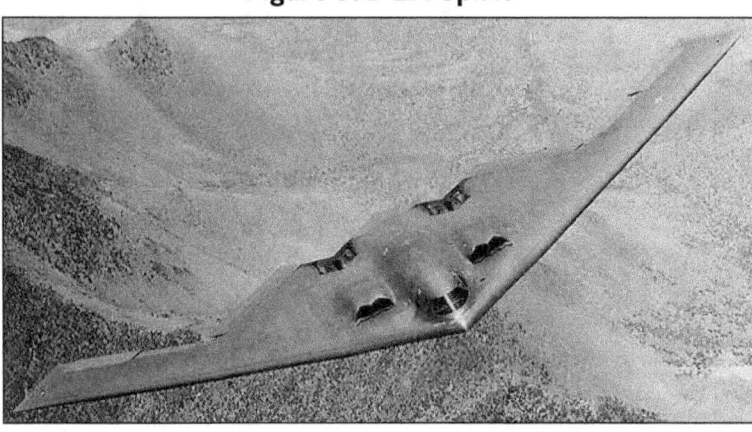

Source: U.S. Air Force official website, B-2 Spirit Factsheet (http://www.af.mil/information/factsheets/).

The B-2A is the only long-range, penetrating low observable (LO) bomber operated by the U.S. Air Force. It serves as both a conventional and nuclear bomber. The aircraft entered service in December 1993 and is based solely at Whiteman AFB, Missouri. It achieved initial operational capability (IOC) in April 1997 and achieved full operational capability (FOC) on December 17, 2003. A total procurement of 132 B-2s was envisioned. However, following the Cold War, the number was reduced to 75, and then to 20. Congress added one more by providing funding to convert one of the test vehicles into a combat aircraft, for a total of 21, but a B-2 was lost in a crash during takeoff at Andersen AFB, Guam, in February 2008, reducing the total number to 20. Its payload weight is more limited than those of the B-1 or B-52. Originally fielded in Block 10 configuration, the current fleet is Block 30.[47] Each block upgrade improved stealth characteristics, expanded weapons employment options, and improved offensive and defensive avionics. Its preeminent capabilities are precision, range, and stealth.

The B-2 currently experiences parts obsolescence and diminishing manufacturing sources. The B-2 is also impacted by aging support and test equipment. For the first time since the B-2 aircraft became fully operational capable, the weapon system's survivability is in question in the face of advancing 21st century A2/AD threats. The B-2A's projected service-life goal is 2058.

Current B-2 Sustainment and Modernization Efforts[48]

The following is a list of B-2 sustainment and modernization initiatives currently in the program of record (POR) that are either just completing or are currently in progress. Additional

---

[46] Information in this section taken from Air Force Global Strike Command's, *B-2 Bomber Master Plan*, June 2012, *Air Force Almanac, May 2012*, and U.S. Air Force B-2 Fact Sheet, April 23, 2010, http://www.af.mil/information/ factsheets/factsheet.asp?fsID=82.

[47] Block refers to essential upgrades to the same model aircraft. Throughout the life of an aircraft, advances in technology create opportunities to upgrade aircraft beyond their original design. This is referred to as a Block upgrade.

[48] Information for current B-1B sustainment and modernization efforts derived from justification books for Air Force procurement accounts and Air Force research, development test and evaluation accounts for FY2013 and prior years.

information on each effort, as well as information on short-term and long-term sustainment and modernization efforts, can be found in the B-2's Master Plan summarized in **Appendix D**.

- Extremely high frequency satellite communications (EHF SATCOM) and computer upgrade program

- Massive ordnance penetrator integration

- Low observable signature and supportability modifications (LOSSM) diagnostics

- B-2 trainer system upgrade

- Link-16/center instrument display/in-flight re-planner (CID/IFR)

- Radar modernization program (RMP)

- Low observable signature and supportability modifications (LOSSM) program structures/materials

- Defensive management system modernization (DMS-M)

- Stores management operational flight program (SMOFP) re-host and mixed carriage modification

- Common very-low frequency receiver (CVR Increment 1)

- Low-cost engine modifications

- Low-cost modifications

- B-2 modernization research, development, test, and evaluation efforts

- Baseline B-2 support

Table 5 is the FY2013 budget submission for B-2 procurement and B-2 research, development, test, and evaluation programs derived from Air Force budget justification books. It summarizes prior-year and estimated future-year expenditures for B-2 sustainment and modernization programs.

Table 5. Current B-2 Sustainment and Modernization Efforts
(in millions of dollars)

Procurement Items	Total Cost All Prior Yrs	Total Cost FY2011	Total Cost FY2012	Total Cost FY2013	Total Cost FY2014	Total Cost FY2015	Total Cost FY2016	Total Cost FY2017	Cost To Complete	Total Cost
EHF SATCOM and Computers	705.523	27.033	29.501	65.037	7.469	8.373	0.000	0.000	0.000	110.380
Massive Ordnance Penetrator Integration	14.887	7.453	0.000	7.000	0.000	0.000	0.000	0.000	0.000	29.340
LOSSM-Diagnostics	0.000	0.000	0.000	2.044	0.741	2.405	2.638	2.131	0.000	9.959
B-2 Trainer System Upgrade	32.331	0.000	0.000	4.038	5.006	6.477	6.630	7.776	0.000	62.258
Link 16/CID/IFR	92.446	0.000	0.000	0.000	0.140	0.100	0.060	0.000	0.000	92.746
Radar System Modification	530.378	8.315	1.210	0.000	0.000	0.000	0.000	0.000	0.000	539.903
LOS and Support Modifications	30.135	16.120	0.000	0.000	0.000	0.000	0.000	0.000	0.000	46.255
Defensive Management System	0.000	0.000	0.000	0.000	0.000	0.000	0.000	0.000	310.933	310.933
LOSSM Structures	0.000	0.000	3.304	2.895	4.089	4.659	4.740	4.901	0.000	21.588
LOSSM Materials	0.000	0.000	0.000	0.516	0.901	1.230	1.430	1.920	0.000	5.997
SMOFP Rehost	0.000	0.000	0.000	0.000	0.000	0.000	12.100	8.900	0.000	21.000
Common Very Low Frequency Terminal	0.000	0.000	0.000	0.000	0.000	0.000	0.000	59.170	12.709	71.879
Low Cost Engine Modifications	6.082	0.599	0.000	0.383	1.631	1.650	1.690	1.718	0.000	13.753
Low Cost Modifications	14.151	1.999	0.000	0.383	2.585	2.615	2.681	2.723	0.000	27.137

B-52 Research, Development, Test & Evaluation: Operational Systems Development

RDT&E Items	Total Cost FY2011	Total Cost FY2012	Total Cost FY2013	Total Cost FY2014	Total Cost FY2015	Total Cost FY2016	Total Cost FY2017	Cost To Complete	Total Cost
B-2 Modernization RDT&E	244.732	27.135	21.759	101.808	101.493	34.544	19.001	Continuing	Continuing
Baseline Support	0.000	9.523	7.875	14.336	16.012	14.032	14.218	Continuing	Continuing
EHF SATCOM and Computer	0.000	202.534	6.336	0.000	0.000	0.000	0.000	Continuing	Continuing
Defensive Management System	0.000	41.127	0.000	0.000	0.000	0.000	0.000	Continuing	Continuing

Source: Prepared by CRS based on justification books for Air Force procurement accounts and Air Force research, development, test, and evaluation accounts for FY2013 and prior years.

Issues for Congress

Potential for Inducing a Shortfall in Long-Range Strike Capabilities

As the bomber force continues to age and shrink, and development of the LRS-B continues, a potential oversight issue for Congress is whether failure to sustain and modernize the Air Force's legacy bomber fleet will induce a shortfall in the nation's long-range strike capabilities. Consistent with prior administrations, the Obama Administration's strategic guidance requires a long-range, deep strike capability that is effective in the face of A2/AD threats and is not constrained by the lack of overseas basing. In addition, under the New START treaty, nuclear-capable heavy bombers could continue to make up one-third of the U.S. nuclear triad along with ICBMs and SLBMs.[49] With only 20 B-2s, the recent retirement of three B-1s, and the conversion of a yet-to-be-determined number of B-52s to conventional-only roles, the potential exists for the total number of bombers to fall below the level necessary to fulfill long-range strike requirements. Currently, the DOD and the Air Force plan on a bomber force of approximately 156 aircraft out to at least 2022 (see **Table 6**, below). However, with $487 billion of defense cuts over the next 10 years as a result of the Budget Control Act of 2011, the potential for additional budget constraints, and changing defense strategies, these numbers are subject to change. Furthermore, the potential for shortfall in long-range strike capabilities does not simply lie in the sheer number of legacy bombers in service.

The more pressing oversight issue is the "capability" of the legacy bomber force. That is, can the legacy bomber force meet the national security challenges posed by the growing number of potential A2/AD-equipped adversaries? The ability of the current bomber force to bridge a potential long-range strike capabilities gap may depend upon the feasibility and cost effectiveness of sustainment and modernization programs that will make these weapon systems viable in the 21st century A2/AD environment while extending their service lives until the LRS-B becomes operational in the late 2020s.

Many analysts argue that the Navy's nuclear-powered aircraft carrier is another, highly flexible alternative to the bomber and is capable of filling the nation's long-range strike needs. Indeed, the aircraft carrier's ability to dominate the seas and launch its aircraft without the need for a forward airbase is without question a valuable strategic asset. However, the relatively limited amount of fuel carried by naval fighters limits their ability to penetrate deeply into enemy territory without assistance from Air Force tankers.[50] Without tanker support, the strategic reach of naval fighters is limited to the coastal areas of any potential adversary. Furthermore, compared to a bomber, the weapons load out capability of carrier-based aircraft is limited thus potentially requiring multiple

---

[49] Department of Defense, *Nuclear Posture Review Report,* April 2010, p 19.

[50] A good example of the challenges faced by carrier aviation is carrier operations during the early stages of Operations Enduring Freedom (OEF) in 2001. Aircraft carriers operating out of the Gulf of Oman and Arabian Sea supplied most of the fighter sorties performing close air support and strike missions as well as supporting airlift and bomber missions during the first few months of the Afghanistan campaign. However, the "short legs" of the naval fighters limited how far north into Afghanistan they could fly. Those naval fighters that did make it further north relied on Air Force tankers (as did many of the other platforms operating in Afghanistan) for multiple refueling and arrived at their tasking with very limited time-on-station and ordinance.

aircraft in order to service a single target. Finally, there is also a potential concern over the carrier's survivability and ability to operate in an A2/AD environment. The primary goal of an adversary employing an anti-access strategy is to deny an outside country the ability to project power into a region. One way of doing this is with anti-ship weapons. Weapons systems such as submarines, China's version of the SS-N-22, SS-N-27, and DF-21D, and Iranian small-boat swarm tactics are all potential threats that could push a carrier task force even further out to sea, thus potentially increasing the range at which naval aviation must travel. Although most analysts will agree the aircraft carrier is an essential element in U.S. long-range strike capabilities, carrier aviation may be seen as complementary to and not taking the place of the much more powerful and flexible long-range bomber. While both capabilities are long-range, they are not necessarily fungible in their military utility.

Table 6. DOD Aviation Long Range Strike Aircraft Inventory (Includes B-52H, B-1B, and B-2)

(FY2013-FY2022)

Inventory	FY12	FY13	FY15	FY16	FY17	FY18	FY19	FY20	FY21	FY22
Long Range Strike	159	158	157	156	156	156	156	156	155	154

Source: Department of Defense, Annual Aviation Inventory and Funding Plan: Fiscal Years (FY) 2013-2042, March 2012, p. 8.

Will Current Air Force Bomber Sustainment and Modernization Plans Get Us to the LRS-B?

Another possible oversight issue for Congress will be the feasibility and affordability of Air Force bomber sustainment and modernization programs and whether those programs bridge any potential capabilities gap until the LRS-B becomes operational. Congress requested such oversight information in the FY2011 National Defense Authorization Act (P.L. 111-383), specifically requesting a report discussing "the cost, schedule, and performance of all planned efforts to modernize and keep viable the existing B-1, B-2, and B-52 bomber fleets and a discussion of the forecasted service-life and all sustainment challenges that the Secretary of the Air Force may confront in keeping those platforms viable until the anticipated retirement of such aircraft." This report was submitted to Congress in September 2011. The information in this report is also contained in Air Force Global Strike Command's (AFGSC's) and Air Combat Command's (ACC's) master plan documents for the B-52 and B-2 (AFGSC) and the B-1 (ACC). Updated on an annual basis, these master plans outline each command's plans, programs, requirements, and strategic vision for each platform to meet national security objectives. The plans also identify timeframes, outline capability needs, and describe the force and technologies needed for continued system effectiveness and viability while providing guidance on long-range sustainment, modernization, and recapitalization needs.

The 2012 updates to these plans take into consideration President Obama's Asia-Pacific rebalance and DOD strategic direction. Primarily, the plans state that without sufficient sustainment and modernization funding, each weapon system's survivability is at risk in the face of 21st century A2/AD threats. **Appendices B** thru **D** provide summaries of each bomber's sustainment and modernization master plans.

To Fund or Not to Fund: What Are DOD and Air Force Priorities?

The DOD is challenged with reducing defense spending by $487 billion over the next 10 years, notwithstanding the possibility of further cuts through possible sequestration. At the same time, the DOD's priorities require continued modernization of aging capabilities to address the proliferation of modern A2/AD threats in that the DOD and Air Force plan on the B-52, B-,1 and B-2 to operate well into the 2030s, especially in the global strike and nuclear deterrent roles.[51] According to DOD's Annual Aviation Inventory and Funding Plan for FY2013-FY2042:

> The enduring need for long-range attack capabilities will be met by a combination of current and future aircraft and weapons systems. The current fleet of Air Force bombers continues to be modernized so that it can retain long range strike capabilities through the 2030s.[52]
>
> The FY12 PB (Presidential Budget) initiated development of the Long-Range Strike-Bomber (LRS-B), a key component of the LRS Family of Systems.... The current goal is to achieve an initial capability in the mid-2020s, and to hold down the unit cost to ensure sufficient production (80 to 100 aircraft) and a sustainable bomber inventory over the long term. Meanwhile, the Department will invest in upgrades to the B-2 bomber to enhance its effectiveness and survivability as well as modernize the B-52 fleet with new visual displays and increased weapons storage capacity. The Air Force also continues to modernize the B-1 and address sustainability issues to ensure the overall health and continued viability of the B-1 fleet.[53]

---

[51] Department of Defense, *Sustaining U.S. Global Leadership: Priorities for 21st Century Defense,* January 2012 (Washington, DC).

[52] Department of Defense, Annual Aviation Inventory and Funding Plan: Fiscal Years (FY) 2013-2042, p. 8.

[53] Ibid. (pdf page 21).

**Figure 6. DOD Planned Long Range Strike Inventories and Funding
(Includes B-52H, B-1B and B-2)**

(FY2013-FY2022)

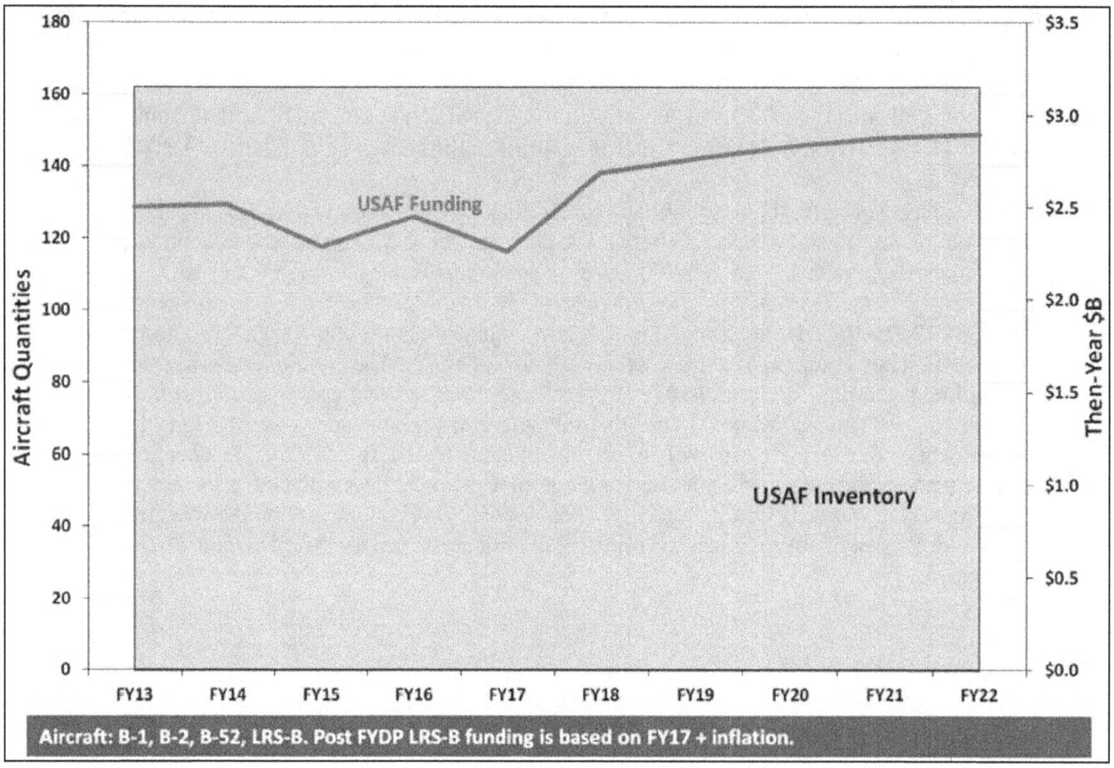

Source: Department of Defense, *Annual Aviation Inventory and Funding Plan: Fiscal Years (FY) 2013–2042,* March 2012, p. 21.

The Air Force's 2012 Posture Statement presented to the House Armed Services Committee suggests funding legacy bomber modernization is a priority given the rise of A2/AD threats.

> The Air Force's ability to conduct global strike—to hold any target on the globe at risk—will be of growing importance in the coming decade. Our conventional strike forces [bombers] compose a significant portion of the Nation's deterrent capability, providing national leaders with a range of crisis response and escalation control options. Our [U.S. Air Force] nuclear deterrent forces provide two-thirds of the Nation's nuclear triad competently forming the foundation of global stability and underwriting our national security and that of our allies. However, increasingly sophisticated air defenses and long-range missile threats require a focused modernization effort exemplified by the long-range strike family of systems.[54]

The posture statement goes on to emphasize that, within the Air Force core functions of Global Precision Attack and Nuclear Deterrence Operations:

> We [the U.S. Air Force] are modernizing conventional bombers to sustain capability while investing in the Long-Range Strike Family of systems. The bomber fleet was retained at its current size because we recognized the importance of long range strike in the current and

---

[54] Department of the U.S. Air Force, *Fiscal Year 2013 Air Force Posture Statement*, Presentation to the Committee on Armed Services United States House of Representatives, February 28, 2012. pp. 4, 5.

future security environments. The Air Force is enhancing long range strike capabilities by upgrading the B-2 fleet with an improved Defensive Management System (DMS) and a new survivable communications system, and is increasing conventional precision guided weapon capacity within the B-52 fleet. We are investing $191.4 million in modernizing the B-1 to prevent obsolescence and diminishing manufacturing sources issues and to help sustain the B-1 to its approximate 2040 service life.[55]

According to the U.S. Air Force's FY2013 Budget Overview:

> The Air Force will continue bomber modernization and sustainment efforts, to include the B-2 Defensive Management systems program, the B-2 Very Low Frequency/Low Frequency communications program, and the B-52 1760 Internal Weapons Bay Upgrades.[56]

> With the February 2011 entry-into-force of the New Strategic Arms Reduction Treaty ... the FY 2013 Budget Request funds compliance activity and force reduction options to meet the central limits of the treaty. These include ... the conversion of some B-52Hs from nuclear-capable to conventional-only capability.[57]

> In addition to the development of LRS-B (Long-Range Strike-Bomber), the Air Force will continue to modernize the B-1B to ensure the fleet remains viable until recapitalization can be accomplished. The FY2013 Budget Request includes the continuation of the B-1 Integrated Battle Station contract which concurrently procures and installs Vertical situation display Upgrade (VSDU), Central Integrated Test System (CITS), and Fully Integrated Data Link (FIDL). VSDU and CITS each address obsolescence and diminishing manufacturing sources for the B-1 fleet. FIDL provides both the electronic backbone for VSDU and CITS, as well as a capability enhancement of line-of-sight/beyond line-of-sight Link 16 communications. In addition, the FY2013 Budget Request includes upgrades to flight and maintenance training devices to ensure continued sustainability and common configuration with the aircraft fleet. These initiatives will help bridge the gap until the next generation long-range strike aircraft is operational.[58]

As Legacy Bombers Phase Out, Are 80-100 LRS-Bs Sufficient?

As the legacy bomber force begins phasing out of service (planned for some time in the mid-2020s thru the 2040s), Congress may want to reevaluate Air Force acquisition plans for the LRS-B to ensure a sufficient backfill of U.S. long-range strike capabilities that meet the requirements of national security objectives. The Air Force and Congress may consider how to balance modernization and sustainment efforts for all three legacy bombers with their gradual phase-out while ensuring a sufficient number of LRS-Bs are produced to minimize the effects of any potential long-range strike capability gap during the transition.

Directly tied to this phase-out/phase-in process will be a final determination by Congress as to the final number of LRS-Bs ultimately produced. Current Air Force plans call for 80-100 LRS-Bs. However, since the 1970s, the number of new combat aircraft actually produced in a given program has rarely come close to the number of aircraft originally planned. In the original 1969

---

[55] Ibid., p. 16.

[56] Department of the U.S. Air Force, *Fiscal Year 2013 Budget Overview*, prepared by the Secretary of the Air Force Office of Financial Management and Budget, February 3, 2012, p. 35.

[57] Ibid., p 36.

[58] Ibid., p 50.

stated requirement, the Air Force planned a production run of 250 B-1A bombers as a replacement for the "then aging" B-52. However, the program was canceled by President Jimmy Carter in 1977; political support for the B-1A waned due to reduced military spending following the Vietnam War and problems within the B-1A program itself. After being revived by President Reagan in 1981, the eventual 100 B-1Bs that were built were the result of an Air Force proposal that split the original 250 B-1As envisioned between 100 B-1Bs and 132 B-2 stealth bombers. Thus, the original 1981 B-2 contract proposed to acquire as many as 132 B-2s. That number was subsequently trimmed to 75 after the end of the Cold War and ultimately only 21 B-2s were built after the program was cancelled in 1991. In fighter aircraft, the Air Force originally sought to acquire 381 F-22 Advanced Tactical Fighters in 2006. However, the resulting high cost of the aircraft ($150 million in FY2009 dollars), a U.S. ban on exports, and the ongoing development of the potentially cheaper and more versatile F-35 resulted in only 195 aircraft built (8 test aircraft and 187 combat aircraft). Currently, the Air Force plans on acquiring 1,763 of the new F-35 Lightning II Joint Strike Fighter. It is yet to be determined if that number will withstand the effects of reductions in defense spending.

Acquisition of anything less than the planned 80-100 LRS-Bs can be expected to drive corresponding modernization and sustainment decisions for the legacy bomber fleet, resulting in further life-extension programs and possibly impacting U.S. long-range strike capabilities, especially in the face of A2/AD equipped adversaries.

If Legacy Bombers are Modernized, Can the Air Force Further Delay Development of the LRS-B?

Another oversight issue for Congress will be whether development of the LRS-B can be further delayed given sufficient levels of funding for legacy bomber sustainment and modernization. Assuming the Air Force makes an effort to keep the B-52 and B-1 operational through 2040 and the B-2 through 2058, it is fair to ask whether the Air Force can further delay development of the LRS-B. All three of the legacy bombers receive meticulous care, with every aspect of their existence recorded and tracked to ensure long-term health and safety of flight. Based on this meticulous care, as well as ongoing structural fatigue testing and computer modeling, the Air Force insists all three bombers will meet their extended service life goals.[59] However, whether the Air Force can further delay development of the LRS-B is not simply a matter of the legacy bombers' air worthiness. With enough funding and continued life extension programs, all three bombers could theoretically fly beyond the Air Force's target dates. Analysts suggest that the real determinant of whether the development of the LRS-B can be further delayed is the legacy bombers' anticipated combat capability over the next 10 to 25 years of operations.

As potential adversaries acquire better and advanced A2/AD defenses, the legacy bombers' ability to get close enough to targets to employ weapons will likely continue to deteriorate. Already, against today's toughest air defenses, the B-52 and B-1 are largely relegated to standoff roles; only the B-2 is expected to get through. In the years to come, the Air Force anticipates the B-2's ability to penetrate will also decline, even though the Air Force plans to upgrade all three bombers with new systems and weapons. According to Air Force Lieutenant General Christopher D. Miller, deputy chief of staff for strategic plans and programs, the current fleet is "increasingly at risk to modernizing air defenses. We need to start now to replace the aging B-52, and B-1

---

[59] John A. Tirpak, "Time to Get Started," *Air Force Magazine*, February 2012, 31.

bomber inventories."[60] When asked whether the steady advance in A2/AD capabilities around the world means the Air Force must have the LRS-B ready for service by a specific deadline, Lieutenant General Miller stated, "I think that decision has been given to us ... Now is the time to get started."[61] As declining defense budgets are anticipated for the foreseeable future, Congress will have to remain cognizant of the actual capabilities realized by funding specific legacy bomber sustainment and modernization efforts with the Air Force's stated requirement to fund and begin LRS-B development now.

Modernization of Bomber-Launched Weapons

Another oversight issue for Congress is the modernization, sustainment, and development of the weapons employed by the legacy bombers—weapons that directly impact their ability to operate in the A2/AD threat environment. As the non-stealthy B-52 and B-1 are likely to operate in the permissive (low-threat) and contested (high-risk) A2/AD employment zones, both platforms will increasingly depend on long-range standoff weapons in order to survive and be effective.

Specifically for the B-52, Congress may consider continued appropriations for the conventional and nuclear capable AGM-86B/C Air Launched Cruise Missile (ALCM) service life extension program (SLEP) and development of a new Advanced Cruise Missile. In her statement before the Senate Foreign Relations Committee in June 2012, Madelyn Creedon, Assistant Secretary of Defense for Global Strategic Affairs, testified,

> Because the growth of modern air defenses is putting even the bomber stand-off missions increasingly at risk, DoD is carrying out an analysis of alternatives (AOA), for a follow-on Air Launched Cruise Missile (ALCM). The final report for the AOA for the new system, the Long-Range Standoff (LRSO) missile, is due in late 2012. The existing ALCM weapon system will be sustained until the LRSO can be fielded during the 2020s.[62]

The AGM-86B/C ALCM started its second SLEP in FY2012 that is intended to extend its service life to 2030. An initial SLEP will be finalized in FY2013 and includes a service life extension of the W80 nuclear warhead.[63] A total of 129 missiles are currently funded for modification with a number being converted into conventional missiles. Congress and the Air Force have also dedicated $887.6 million from FY2011 to FY2016 to the development of a new Advanced Cruise Missile that will ultimately replace the AGM-86 family of ALCMs. In FY2012, Air Force research and development funds were transferred from the AGM-86 to "Nuclear Modernization" to identify viable concepts and solutions to replace the AGM-86.[64]

For both the B-52 and the B-1, the acquisition, test and evaluation, and fielding of the Miniature Air Launched Decoy (MALD) and MALD-J (jammer) would enhance the ability of these aircraft

---

[60] Ibid.,

[61] Ibid., 35.

[62] Testimony of Ms. Madelyn Creedon, Assistant Secretary of Defense for Global Strategic Affairs, in Senate, *Hearings before the Senate Foreign Relations Committee*, 112th Congress, 2nd Session, June 21, 2012.

[63] The W80 is a small thermonuclear warhead with a variable yield of between 5 and 150 kiloton of TNT. It was designed for deployment on cruise missiles and is the warhead used in the majority of nuclear-armed USAF ALCMs.

[64] The Center for Arms Control and Non-Proliferation, *Air Launched Cruise Missile Fact Sheet*, http://armscontrolcenter.org/assets/pdfs/ALCMFactSheet.pdf and United States Air Force, *Department of Defense FY2012 President's Budget Submission, Missile Procurement*, http://www.saffm hq.af.mil/budget/.

to operate in contested (high-risk) and highly contested (extreme-risk) A2/AD employment zones. MALD and MALD-J are designed to present a realistic decoy representing penetrating fighter, attack, and bomber aircraft to enemy integrated air defense systems (IADS). MALD-J incorporates a jammer while retaining the decoy capabilities. The B-52 is the initial demonstration platform for this program and is currently undergoing initial operational test and evaluation with initial operational capability scheduled for early 2013. The B-1 community is exploring further integration of MALD and MALD-J on the B-1.

For all three legacy bombers, continued acquisition of the AGM-158A Joint Air-Surface Standoff Missile (JASSM) and the AGM-158B JASSM-ER (extended range) and the development of the Long-Range Anti-Ship Missile (LRASM) is considered by some analysts essential to their effectiveness in future A2/AD environments. The JASSM provides a long-range, conventional air-to-surface, autonomous, precision guided, standoff cruise missile able to attack a variety of fixed or re-locatable targets. The Air Force plans on procuring 4,900 missiles (2,400 baseline versions and 2,500 ER) with an estimated program cost of $6.1 billion beyond FY2017.[65] In addition to the JASSM, the Defense Advanced Research Projects Agency (DARPA), in partnership with Lockheed Martin, is developing the LRASM. It stems from a 2008 urgent operational needs statement from the U.S. Pacific Fleet requesting weapons technology to defeat heavily defended ship targets. LRASM includes a datalink to provide updates as the missile approaches the target area and an anti-radiation homing capability to detect and identify emissions from threats to help guide the missile to the target. This long-range, anti-ship capability dovetails with the U.S. rebalance to the Asia-Pacific region and may prove invaluable in any maritime conflict as potential adversaries continue to equip their naval vessels with highly advanced weapon systems. LRASM is based on the AGM-158B JASSM and has an unclassified range of 500 nautical miles. Lockheed Martin and the Air Force are planning to test-fire three LRASM missiles in 2013 from the B-1B.[66]

Potential Implications of Bomber Modernization on Air Force Basing and any Future Base Realignment and Closures (BRAC)

Another potential oversight issue is the potential implications of reduced bomber sustainment and modernization, and subsequent diminishing numbers of airframes, on any future rounds of base realignment and closure (BRAC) efforts. Although the DOD included two rounds of BRAC in its 2013 budget proposal, Congress did not authorize any closures or realignments. However, as the DOD continues to look for ways to divest itself of assets in an effort to meet budgetary challenges, BRAC continues to be a subject of speculation, possibly as early as 2015.[67]

The legacy bomber force is not getting bigger. The original 744 B-52s built were stationed at approximately 21 bases across the United States during the height of the Cold War. There are now 76 B-52Hs in service stationed at two bases, Barksdale AFB, Louisiana, and Minot AFB, North

---

[65] United States Air Force, *Department of Defense FY2013 President's Budget Submission, Missile Procurement*, http://www.saffm hq.af.mil/shared/media/document/AFD-120207-052.pdf, p 49.

[66] Grace Jean, *Long-Range Anti-Ship Missile Poised for Air Launch Tests, Possible Ship Integration* (Defense & Security Intelligence & Analysis: HIS Jane's, September 20, 2012), http://www.janes.com/products/janes/defence-security-report.aspx?id=1065971576.

[67] Henry Cuningham, *New BRAC Round Looming* (Fayetteville (N.C.) Observer, December 23, 2012), http://www military.com/daily-news/2012/12/23/new-brac-round-looming.html

Dakota. The original 100 B-1s built in the 1980s were stationed at six bases from 1986 until 2001. Now, there are 63 B-1s stationed at two bases, Dyess AFB, Texas, and Ellsworth AFB, South Dakota. All four of these bases have excess capacity with the potential to accommodate the entire B-52 fleet at either Barksdale or Minot and the entire B-1 fleet at Dyess or Ellsworth. If the current trend of retiring airframes to pay for sustainment and modernization efforts continues (as was done with the B-1 when 27 aircraft in 2001-2002 and three aircraft in 2012 were retired in order to use the savings to pay for sustainment and upgrades), the total fleet size of both bombers may suggest consolidation at one base simply from a cost feasibility perspective.

Ellsworth AFB in South Dakota survived the 2005 BRAC when the federal base-closing commission voted to keep the base open, despite Pentagon recommendations to close the base and consolidate the B-1 fleet at Dyess AFB in Texas. Ellsworth employs some 4,000 people and has an estimated economic impact of $278 million on the local community.[68] Although no BRAC actions were taken for Minot AFB and Barksdale AFB in 2005, Air Force BRAC planners initially proposed retiring Minot's 150 Minuteman III intercontinental ballistic missiles and realigning the base. Ultimately, planners decided this idea would not work and the Air Force's top BRAC committee, the Base Closure Executive Group, rejected the idea.[69] As far as the B-2 is concerned, all 20 are stationed at Whiteman AFB, Missouri. There has been no public discussion of potential basing for the LRS-B, if and when it finally hits the flight line in the mid-to-late 2020s.

Industrial Base Concerns Associated with Bomber Sustainment

Another oversight issue is the ability of the nation's industrial base to sustain the legacy bomber force. A potential problem with sustaining a fleet of bombers with an average age of 33 years is that the industrial base that developed and produced these aircraft may no longer possess the capability to manufacture and supply parts in necessary quantities—if at all—to affordably keep these aircraft flying. Especially in the case of the B-52 and B-1, many of the original parts designed and produced in the 1950s (for the B-52) and the 1970s (for the B-1) are simply not produced anymore. Both airframes struggle with diminishing manufacturing sources and material shortages in an effort to replace and repair aircraft parts and equipment that the original manufactures do not make anymore. As the nation's current budget deficit debate shifts from taxes towards spending cuts and the debt limit, commentators note the potential for deep defense cuts may drive the defense industry to streamline and consolidate operations, potentially exit prior production lines, and undergo internal restructuring in an effort to maintain their existing profit margins. Consequently, a question to be answered is whether the defense industrial base will even be capable of meeting the sustainment requirements of America's legacy bomber force out to 2040 and to what extent Congress should consider this issue when evaluating proposed defense cuts.

---

[68] Bob Reha, *South Dakota's Ellsworth AFB to Say Open* (Minnesota Public Radio, August 26, 2005), http://news.minnesota.publicradio.org/features/2005/08/26_rehab_ellsworthopen/

[69] Nicole Gaudiano, *Air Force BRAC Planners Nixed Minot Realignment* (Air Force Times, September 5, 2005), http://www.airforcetimes.com/legacy/new/0-AIRPAPER-1034249.php

Historical Appropriations for Bomber Sustainment and Modernization, FY2002-2012

Figure 7 depicts historical authorizations and appropriations for B-52H, B-1B, and B-2 sustainment and modernization. Dollar amounts include funds authorized/appropriated in the "Procurement" and "Research, Development, Test and Evaluation" sections as well as any funds authorized/appropriated for sustainment and modernization efforts directly tied to "Overseas Contingency Operations" provided for in National Defense Authorization and Appropriations acts from FY2002 to FY2013. **Figure 8** is a side-by-side graphical comparison of historical appropriations for all three bombers.

Figure 9 is an overlay of historical appropriations for all three bombers and their average yearly mission capable rate. Mission capable rate is defined as the percentage of aircraft in each of the bomber fleet components that are capable of performing its intended wartime mission.

Figure 7. Congressional Authorizations and Appropriations for Bomber Sustainment and Modernization

(in millions of "then-year" dollars, rounded to nearest tenth)

	B-52		B-1		B-2	
	Authorized	**Appropriated**	**Authorized**	**Appropriated**	**Authorized**	**Appropriated**
FY02	70.4	110.7	296.4	196.4	281.5	293.1
FY03	65.8	111.5	260.7	276.4	406.2	406.2
FY04	89.8	117.4	194.1	200.9	352.3	329.1
FY05	137.4	188.3	254.4	259.4	408.5	408.5
FY06	241	255.5	226.8	182.4	393.8	387.8
FY07	205.4	204.3	196.1	196.1	450.9	453.2
FY08	138.2	142.7	178.8	187.8	536.2	546.2
FY09	80.4	80.4	168.7	168.7	728.9	728.9
FY10	155.4	163.8	280	261.5	735.9	699.3
FY11	218.6	199.2	248.6	252.1	350.1	350.1
FY12	187.9	187.9	235.8	235.8	371.1	360.8
FY13	63.0	63.0	167.0	167.0	447.0	447.0

Sources: National Defense Authorization Acts, Appropriation Acts, and Committee Reports for Fiscal Years 2002 to 2013. Dollar amounts include procurement and research, development, test, and evaluation funding.

Figure 8. B-52, B-1 and B-2 Appropriations Comparison

(in "then-year" dollars)

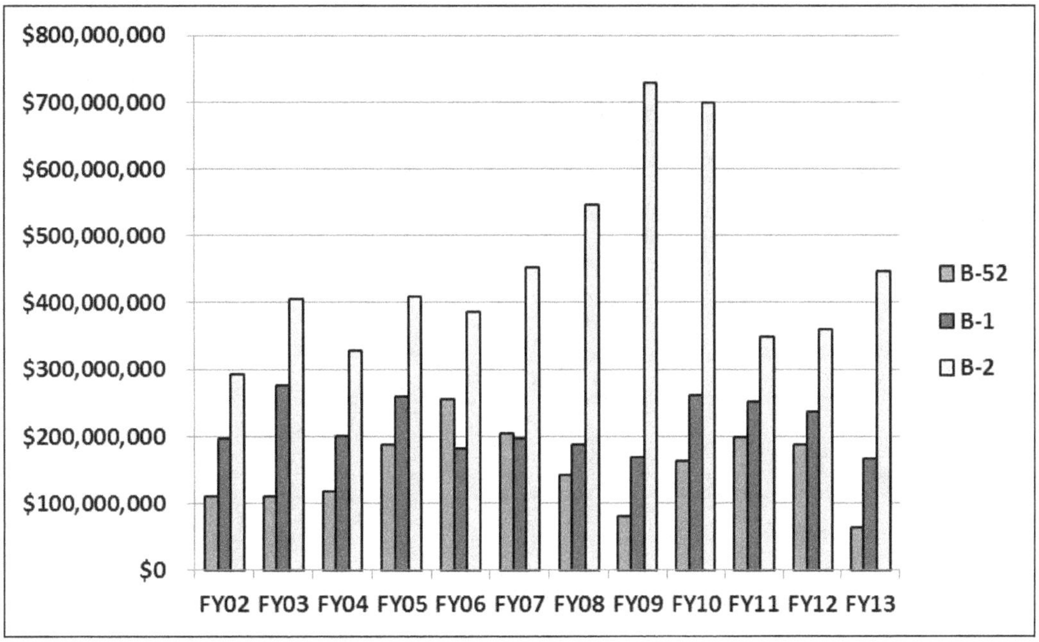

Sources: National Defense Authorization Acts, Appropriation Acts, and Committee Reports for Fiscal Years 2002 to 2013.

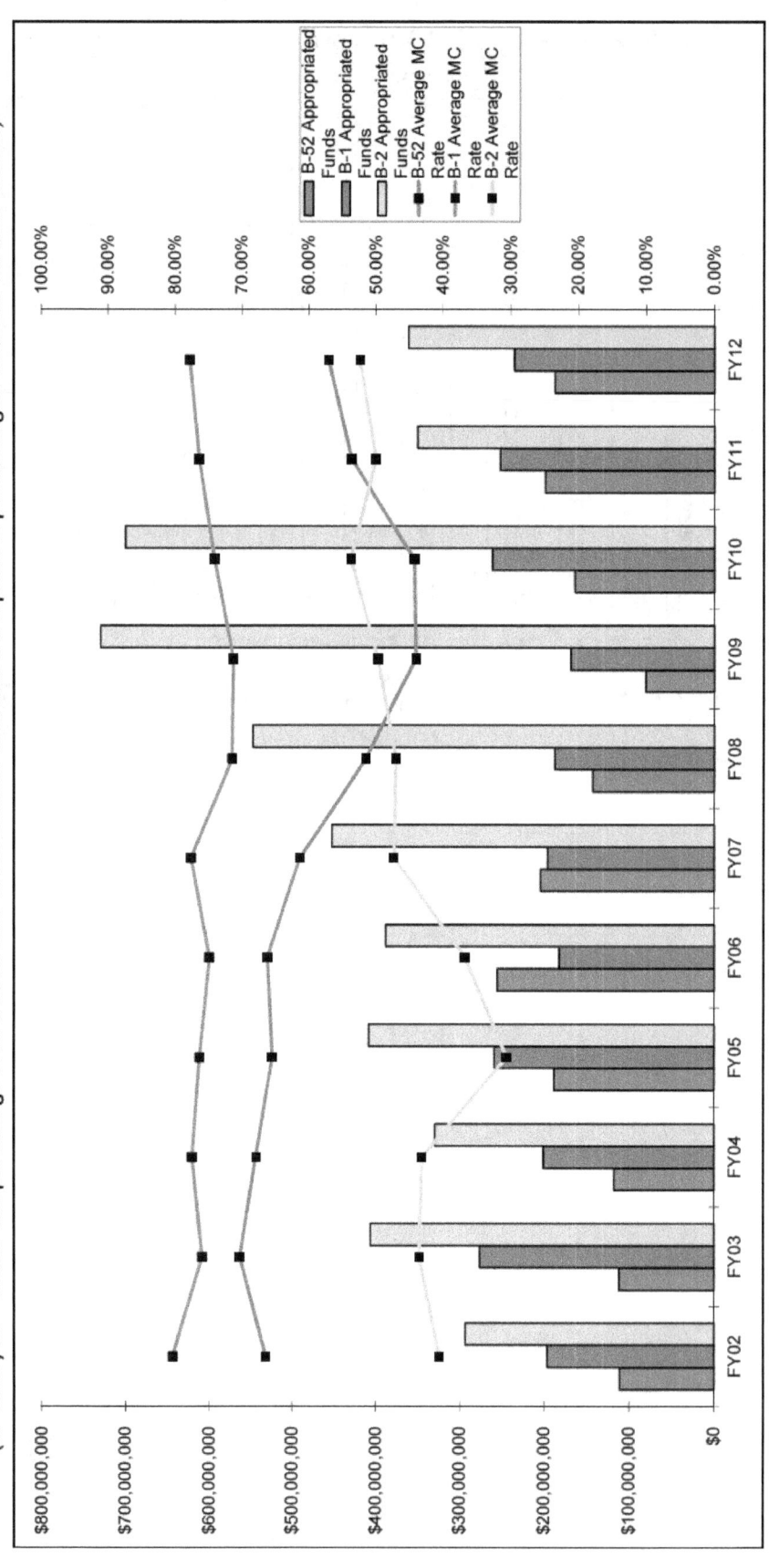

Figure 9. B-52, B-1 and B-2 Appropriations and Average Historical Mission Capable Rates

(in "then-year" dollars and percentage of aircraft in each of the bomber fleet that are capable of performing its intended wartime mission)

Source: National Defense Authorization Acts, Appropriation Acts, and Committee Reports for Fiscal Years 2002 to 2013 and mission capable rates as reported to Headquarters U.S. Air Force by Air Combat Command and Global Strike Command.

Legislative Activity FY2011-FY2013

The follow is a brief summary of legislative actions involving U.S. Air Force bomber sustainment and modernization from fiscal years 2011 through 2013. It also highlights Congress's interest in the potential threat posed by countries seeking to implement anti-access/area denial capabilities and strategies. The complete legislative language for each of these efforts can be found in **Appendix E**.

FY2011 National Defense Authorization Act (P.L. 111-383)

Section 1056 of **P.L. 111-383** directed the Secretary of the Air Force to submit to congressional defense committees a report concerning bomber modernization, sustainment, and recapitalization efforts in support of the National Defense Strategy. In the report, the Air Force was to discuss the cost, schedule, and performance of all planned efforts to modernize and keep viable the existing B–1, B–2, and B–52 bomber fleets. Congress also requested the forecasted service-life and all sustainment challenges that the Secretary of the Air Force may confront in keeping those platforms viable until the anticipated retirement of all three aircraft. As previously discussed, this report was submitted to Congress in September 2011 and contains similar information as that found in the Air Force Global Strike Command's (AFGSC's) and Air Combat Command's (ACC's) master plan documents for the B-52 and B-2 (AFGSC) and the B-1 (ACC) presented in **Appendixes B** through **D**.

Under **Section 1238** of **P.L. 111-383**, Congress requested an additional report on United States' efforts to defend against threats posed by the Anti-Access and Area-Denial capabilities of certain nations-states. This report was requested in response to DOD's 2010 Quadrennial Defense Review that concluded "[a]nti-access strategies seek to deny outside countries the ability to project power into a region, thereby allowing aggression or other destabilizing actions to be conducted by the anti-access powers. Without dominant capabilities to project power, the integrity of United States alliances and security partnerships could be called into question, reducing United States security and influence and increasing the possibility of conflict." Congress also requested an assessment by the Secretary of Defenses on the United States' efforts to defend against any potential future threats posed by the anti-access and area-denial capabilities of potentially hostile nation-states. These reports were submitted to the House and Senate Armed Services Committees in April 2011.

FY2012 Department of Defense Appropriations (H.Rept. 112-331)

In the DOD's FY2012 budget request, the Air Force proposed the retirement of six B-1 bombers with the intent of putting the money saved by retiring these aircraft towards modernization and sustainment efforts for the remaining 60 B-1 aircraft. In response to this proposal, the House Appropriations Committee made the following recommendation in their conference report to accompany H.R. 2055.

> The fiscal year 2012 budget request includes a proposal to retire six B–1 bomber aircraft. The conferees understand that the B– 1 fleet continues to operate almost constantly over Afghanistan in support of troops on the ground and that the B–1 is a critical component of the Nation's long-range strike capabilities. The Air Force proposed to reinvest less than 40

percent of the savings from aircraft retirements in the B–1 modernization program across the Future Years Defense Program. The conferees are concerned that premature retirement of six B–1 aircraft could negatively impact long-range strike capabilities. Therefore, the conferees direct the Secretary of the Air Force to reinvest a larger portion of savings realized from B–1 aircraft retirements, to the extent authorized by law, in the sustainment and modernization of the B–1 fleet.

FY2012 National Defense Authorization Act (P.L. 112-81)

Further responding to the Air Force's proposal to retire six B-1s, **Section 132** in **P.L. 112-81** sought to clarify the Air Force's plan by restricting FY2012 funds for the retirement of any B-1 aircraft until the Secretary of the Air Force submitted a plan to congressional defense committees detailing the following:

- Identification of each B–1 bomber aircraft that will be retired and the disposition plan for such aircraft;

- an estimate of the savings that will result from the proposed retirement of B–1 bomber aircraft in each calendar year through calendar year 2022;

- an estimate of the amount of the savings that will be reinvested in the modernization of B–1 bomber aircraft still in service in each calendar year through calendar year 2022;

- a modernization plan for sustaining the remaining B–1 bomber aircraft through at least calendar year 2022; and,

- an estimate of the amount of funding required to fully fund the modernization plan for each calendar year through calendar year 2022.

Language in **Section 132** also went on to specify that if retirement of six B-1s was justified, after subsequently retiring those aircraft, the Secretary of the Air Force will maintain in a common capability configuration no less than 36 combat-coded B–1 aircraft out to September 30, 2013.[70] After that date, no less than 35 combat-coded aircraft until September 30, 2014, then 34 until September 30, 2015, and finally 33 combat-coded aircraft until September 30, 2016.[71]

Section 134 of **P.L. 112-81** made available certain FY2011 funds for research and development relating to the B-2 bomber. Specifically, $20 million was made available for FY2012 for research, development, test and evaluation of a conventional weapons mixed load capability for the B–2. In addition, **Section 135** made available $15 million of FY2011 funds for research, development, test and evaluation of alternative options for the B-2's extremely high frequency terminal Increment 1 program of record.[72]

---

[70] Combat-coded aircraft is defined as aircraft assigned to meet the primary aircraft authorization to a unit for the performance of its wartime mission.

[71] As of this writing, the Air Force has retired only three of the originally proposed six B-1s.

[72] The B-2 Extremely High Frequency (EHF) satellite communications (SATCOM) program supports the replacement of the B-2's ultra-high-frequency radio terminal set with an EHF SATCOM system that will be compatible with the military's legacy MILSTAR I/II satellite constellation and the future AEHF satellite constellation.

FY2013 Department of Defense Appropriations (S.Rept. 112-196: To accompany H.R. 5856)

Note: as of this writing, this legislation has not been passed into law.

The FY2013 budget request did not include funds under Aircraft Procurement for the B-52 CONECT program of record due to the Air Force's decision to terminate the program.[73] Instead, it included $34,700,000 for research, development, test and evaluation for a restructured and descoped B–52 CONECT program. The committee, however, directed that no funds may be obligated or expended for the B–52 CONECT program of record post-milestone C acquisition activities or for a restructured B–52 CONECT program until 30 days after the congressional defense committees have been briefed on the Air Force's proposed way ahead.

The committee also addressed the Air Force's decision to terminate the B-52 Strategic Radar Replacement [SR2] program. The B-52's existing APQ-166 radar was produced in the 1960s, has a 20 to 30 hour mean-time between failure rate, has limited in capabilities, and is costly to operate and maintain. Although the Air Force conducted a lengthy analysis of alternatives in 2011 and ultimately terminated the program, the committee encouraged the Secretary of the Air Force to reconsider this decision.

FY2013 Department of Defense Authorizations (P.L. 112-239)

The subject of retiring B-1 aircraft was addressed again in **P.L. 112-239**. **Section 142** amended Section 8062 of title 10, United States Code, by adding at the end a new subsection stating, "Beginning October 1, 2011, the Secretary of the Air Force may not retire more than six B–1 aircraft" and "shall maintain in a common capability configuration not less than 36 B–1 aircraft as combat-coded aircraft."

Section 211 addressed concerns over the nuclear certification requirements of the Air Force's proposed Next-Generation Bomber by directing the Secretary of the Air Force to ensure the next-generation long-range strike bomber is capable of carrying nuclear weapons as of the date on which the aircraft achieves initial operating capability (IOC) and is also certified to use such weapons no later than two years after IOC.

Conclusion

In the wake of fiscal constraints levied by the Budget Control Act of 2011 (P.L. 112-25/S. 365) and the implementation of sequestration on March 1, 2013, Congress and the Air Force will be faced with difficult decisions regarding fiscal appropriations for bomber sustainment and modernization. The impacts of these fiscal measures on bomber appropriations can already be seen with implementation of the FY2013 defense budget. From FY2002 through FY2012, the sustainment and modernization appropriations for the B-52, B-1, and B-2 averaged $160.15

---

[73] The B-52 Combat Network Communications Technology (CONECT) acquisition program supports nuclear and conventional operations by upgrading the B-52 fleet with tactical datalink and voice communications capability along with improved threat and situational awareness to support participation in network centric operations.

million, $219.77 million, and $451.2 million per year respectively. For the FY2013 budget, appropriations for the B-52 were $63 million, down 61% from the prior 11-year average and the lowest amount appropriated since FY2002. FY2013 appropriations for the B-1 were $167 million, down 24% from the prior 11-year average and also the lowest amount appropriated since FY2002. The B-2 was the only bomber not affected by the budget cuts in FY2013 with $447 million appropriated, a drop of only 1% from the prior 11-year average. Meanwhile, potential foes and long-time allies in the Asia-Pacific are undergoing major (in some cases unprecedented) expansions of their defense capabilities in order to secure or expand their diplomatic, economic, and strategic influence in the region. The result is an increase in the proliferation of advanced 21st century weapon systems and a trend of countries adopting A2/AD strategies to secure their national interests. Nevertheless, time and time again, the United States turns to its long-range bomber force as means of flexing its deterrent muscle, as it did most recently in response to renewed threats of war by North Korean leader Kim Jong Un. In March and April of 2013, the United States sent B-52s and B-2s on short-notice deployments for exercises with South Korean forces and for shows-of-force over the Korean peninsula as a visible signal to Kim Jong Un that such threats by the North's regime will not go unchecked. However, as potential A2/AD equipped adversaries throughout the world become more prevalent and more capable, the question remains: will the Air Force's legacy bomber force keep pace with sustainment and modernization efforts in order to remain a credible response to such adversaries, or will they become increasingly irrelevant because the nation cannot afford them? In large part, decisions by Congress will determine just how much longer the B-52, B-1, and B-2 will remain relevant, and ultimately, will likely determine the future of the nation's long-range strike capabilities.

Appendix A. Existing Bomber Force

This appendix presents additional information on the U.S. Air Force's existing fleet of B-52H, B-1B, and B-2 bombers.

52H Stratofortress[74]

Mission

The B-52H is a long-range, heavy bomber that can perform a variety of missions. The bomber is capable of flying at high subsonic speeds at altitudes up to 50,000 feet (15,166.6 meters). It can carry nuclear or precision guided conventional ordnance with worldwide precision navigation capability.

Features

In a conventional conflict, the B-52H can perform strategic attack, close-air support, air interdiction, offensive counter-air, and maritime operations. During Desert Storm, B-52s delivered 40% of all the weapons dropped by coalition forces. It is also capable of ocean surveillance, and can assist the U.S. Navy in anti-ship and mine-laying operations. Two B-52Hs, in two hours, can monitor 140,000 square miles (364,000 square kilometers) of ocean surface.

All B-52Hs can be equipped with two electro-optical viewing sensors, a forward-looking infrared camera, and an advanced targeting pod, to augment targeting, battle assessment, and flight safety.

Pilots wear night vision goggles, or NVGs, to enhance their vision during night operations. Night vision goggles provide greater safety during night operations by increasing the pilot's ability to visually clear terrain, avoid enemy radar, and see other aircraft in a lights-out environment.

Starting in 1989, on-going modifications incorporate the global positioning system, heavy stores adapter beams for carrying 2,000 pound munitions, and a full array of advance weapons currently under development.

The use of aerial refueling gives the B-52H a range limited only by crew endurance. It has an unrefueled combat range in excess of 8,800 miles (14,080 kilometers).

Background

The B-52H is capable of dropping or launching a wide array of weapons. This includes gravity bombs, cluster bombs, precision guided missiles, and joint direct attack munitions. Updated with modern technology the B-52H will be capable of delivering the full complement of joint developed weapons. Current engineering analyses show the B-52H's life span to extend beyond the year 2040.

---

[74] Information in this section comes from the U.S. Air Force Fact Sheet for the B-52H Stratofortress, December 4, 2012, http://www.af mil/information/factsheets/factsheet.asp?id=83.

The B-52A first flew in 1954, and the B model entered service in 1955. A total of 744 B-52s were built with the last, a B-52H, delivered in October 1962. The first of 102 B-52Hs was delivered to Strategic Air Command in May 1961. The H model can carry up to 20 air launched cruise missiles. In addition, it can carry the conventional cruise missile that was launched in several contingencies during the 1990s, starting with Operation Desert Storm and culminating with Operation Iraqi Freedom.

In Operations Desert Storm and Allied Force, B-52s struck wide-area troop concentrations, fixed installations and bunkers, and decimated the morale of Iraq's Republican Guard. On September 2 and 3, 1996, two B-52H's struck Baghdad power stations and communications facilities with 13 AGM-86C conventional air launched cruise missiles, or CALCMs, as part of Operation Desert Strike. At the time, this mission was the longest distance flown for a combat mission, involving a 34-hour, 16,000 statute mile, round trip from Barksdale Air Force Base, LA.

In 2001, the B-52H contributed to Operation Enduring Freedom by loitering high above the battlefield and providing close air support through the use of precision guided munitions.

The B-52H also played a role in Operation Iraqi Freedom. On March 21, 2003, B-52Hs launched approximately 100 CALCMs during a night mission.

Only the H model is still in the Air Force inventory and is assigned to the 5th Bomb Wing at Minot AFB, ND, and the 2nd Bomb Wing at Barksdale AFB, LA, which fall under Air Force Global Strike Command. The aircraft is also assigned to the Air Force Reserve Command's 307th Bomb Wing at Barksdale.

General Characteristics
Primary Function: Heavy bomber
Contractor: Boeing Military Airplane Co.
Power plant: Eight Pratt & Whitney engines TF33-P-3/103 turbofan
Thrust: Each engine up to 17,000 pounds
Wingspan: 185 feet (56.4 meters)
Length: 159 feet, 4 inches (48.5 meters)
Height: 40 feet, 8 inches (12.4 meters)
Weight: Approximately 185,000 pounds (83,250 kilograms)
Maximum Takeoff Weight: 488,000 pounds (219,600 kilograms)
Fuel Capacity: 312,197 pounds (141,610 kilograms)
Payload: 70,000 pounds (31,500 kilograms)
Speed: 650 miles per hour (Mach 0.86)
Range: 8,800 miles (7,652 nautical miles)
Ceiling: 50,000 feet (15,151.5 meters)
Armament: Approximately 70,000 pounds (31,500 kilograms) mixed ordnance—bombs, mines, and missiles. (Modified to carry air-launched cruise missiles)
Crew: Five (aircraft commander, pilot, radar navigator, navigator, and electronic warfare officer)
Unit Cost: $53.4 million (FY1998 constant dollars)
Initial operating capability: April 1952
Inventory: Active force, 76; ANG, 0; Reserve, 9

B-1B Lancer[75]

Mission

Carrying the largest payload of both guided and unguided weapons in the Air Force inventory, the multi-mission B-1 can rapidly deliver massive quantities of precision and non-precision weapons.

Features

The B-1B's blended wing and body configuration, variable-geometry wings, and turbofan afterburning engines combine to provide long range, maneuverability, and high speed while enhancing survivability. Forward wing settings are used for takeoff, landings, air refueling, and in some high-altitude weapons employment scenarios. Aft wing sweep settings—the main combat configuration—are typically used during high subsonic and supersonic flight, enhancing the B-1B's maneuverability in the low- and high-altitude regimes. The B-1B's speed and handling characteristics, large payload, radar targeting system, long loiter time, and survivability allow it to integrate with almost any joint/composite strike force.

The B-1B is a multi-mission weapon system. Its synthetic aperture radar is capable of tracking, targeting, and engaging moving vehicles as well as self-targeting and terrain-following modes. In addition, an extremely accurate Global Positioning System-aided Inertial Navigation System enables aircrews to navigate without the aid of ground-based navigation aids as well as engage targets with a high level of precision. Combat Track II data link radios provide a secure, beyond-line-of-sight reach back connectivity for command and control and in-flight re-tasking/re-targeting. In a time sensitive targeting environment, the aircrew can use targeting data from the Combined Air Operations Center over Combat Track II to strike emerging targets.

The B-1B's onboard self-protection electronic jamming equipment, radar warning receiver, expendable countermeasures, and a towed decoy system complement its low-radar cross-section to form an integrated defense system that supports penetration of hostile airspace. The electronic countermeasures system detects and identifies adversary threat radars and then applies the appropriate jamming technique either automatically or through operator inputs.

Current B-1B sustainment and modernization efforts build on this foundation. Radar sustainability and capability upgrades will provide a more reliable system and may be upgraded in the future to include an ultra-high-resolution capability and automatic target recognition. The addition of a fully integrated data link, or FIDL, will add Link-16 line-of-sight data link communications capability. FIDL combined with associated cockpit upgrades will provide the crew with a much more flexible, integrated cockpit. Several obsolete and hard to maintain electronic systems are also being replaced to improve aircraft reliability.

Background

The B-1A was initially developed in the 1970s as a replacement for the B-52. Four prototypes of this long-range, high speed (Mach 2.2) strategic bomber were developed and tested in the mid-

---

[75] Information in this section comes from the U.S. Air Force Fact Sheet for the B-1B Lancer, May 21, 2012, http://www.af mil/information/factsheets/factsheet.asp?fsID=81.

1970s, but the program was canceled in 1977 before going into production. Flight testing continued through 1981.

The B-1B is an improved variant initiated by the Reagan Administration in 1981. Major changes included the addition of additional structure to increase payload by 74,000 pounds, an improved radar, and reduction of the aircraft's radar cross section (RCS) by an order of magnitude. The engine inlets were extensively modified as part of this RCS reduction, necessitating a reduction in maximum speed to Mach 1.2.

The first production B-1B flew in October 1984, and the first aircraft was delivered to Dyess Air Force Base, Texas, in June 1985. Initial operational capability was achieved on October 1, 1986. The final B-1B was delivered May 2, 1988.

The B-1B was first used in combat in support of operations against Iraq during Operation Desert Fox in December 1998. In 1999, six B-1Bs were used in Operation Allied Force, delivering more than 20% of the total ordnance while flying less than 2% of the combat sorties.

During the first six months of Operation Enduring Freedom, eight B-1Bs dropped nearly 40% of the total tonnage delivered by coalition air forces. This included nearly 3,900 Joint Direct Attack Munitions (JDAMs), or 67% of the total. In Operation Iraqi Freedom, the aircraft flew less than 1% of the combat missions while delivering 43% of the JDAMs used. The B-1 continues to be deployed today, flying missions daily in support of continuing operations.

General Characteristics
Primary Function: Long-range, multi-role, heavy bomber
Contractor: Boeing, North America (formerly Rockwell International, North American Aircraft); Offensive avionics, Boeing Military Airplane; defensive avionics, EDO Corporation
Power plant: Four General Electric F101-GE-102 turbofan engine with afterburner
Thrust: 30,000-plus pounds with afterburner, per engine
Wingspan: 137 feet (41.8 meters) extended forward, 79 feet (24.1 meters) swept aft
Length: 146 feet (44.5 meters)
Height: 34 feet (10.4 meters)
Weight: approximately 190,000 pounds (86,183 kilograms)
Maximum Takeoff Weight: 477,000 pounds (216,634 kilograms)
Fuel Capacity: 265,274 pounds (120,326 kilograms)
Payload: 75,000 pounds (34,019 kilograms)
Speed: 900-plus mph (Mach 1.2 at sea level)
Range: Intercontinental
Ceiling: More than 30,000 feet (9,144 meters)
Armament: 84 500-pound Mk-82 or 24 2,000-pound Mk-84 general purpose bombs; up to 84 500-pound Mk-62 or 8 2,000-pound Mk-65 Quick Strike naval mines; 30 cluster munitions (CBU-87, -89, -97) or 30 Wind-Corrected Munitions Dispensers (CBU-103, -104, -105); up to 24 2,000-pound GBU-31 or 15 500-pound GBU-38 Joint Direct Attack Munitions; up to 24 AGM-158A Joint Air-to-Surface Standoff Missiles; GBU-54 Laser Joint Direct Attack Munition
Crew: Four (aircraft commander, copilot, and two weapon systems officers)
Unit Cost: $283.1 million (fiscal 98 constant dollars)
Initial operating capability: October 1986
Inventory: Active force, 63 (test, 2); ANG, 0; Reserve, 0

B-2 Spirit[76]

Mission

The B-2 Spirit is a multi-role bomber capable of delivering both conventional and nuclear munitions.

Features

Along with the B-52H and the B-1B, the B-2 provides the penetrating flexibility and effectiveness inherent in manned bombers. Its low-observable, or "stealth," characteristics give it the ability to penetrate an enemy's most sophisticated defenses and threaten its most valued, and heavily defended, targets.

The blending of low-observable technologies with high aerodynamic efficiency and large payload gives the B-2 important advantages over existing bombers. Its low observability provides it greater freedom of action at high altitudes, thus increasing its range and providing a better field of view for the aircraft's sensors. Its unrefueled range is approximately 6,000 nautical miles (9,600 kilometers).

The B-2's low observability is derived from a combination of reduced infrared, acoustic, electromagnetic, visual, and radar signatures. These signatures make it difficult for sophisticated defensive systems to detect, track, and engage the B-2. Many aspects of the low observability process remain classified; however, the B-2's composite materials, special coatings, and flying-wing design all contribute to its "stealthiness."

The B-2 has a crew of two pilots: an aircraft commander in the left seat and a mission commander in the right.

Background

The first B-2 was publicly displayed on November 22, 1988, when it was rolled out of its hangar at Air Force Plant 42, Palmdale, CA. Its first flight was July 17, 1989. The B-2 Combined Test Force, Air Force Flight Test Center, Edwards Air Force Base, CA, is responsible for flight testing, engineering, manufacturing, and development of the B-2.

Whiteman AFB, MO, is the only operational base for the B-2. The first aircraft, Spirit of Missouri, was delivered December 17, 1993. Depot maintenance responsibility for the B-2 is performed by Air Force contractor support and is managed at the Oklahoma City Air Logistics Center at Tinker AFB, OK.

In Operation Allied Force, the B-2 was responsible for destroying 33% of all Serbian targets in the first eight weeks, by flying nonstop to Kosovo from its home base in Missouri and back. In support of Operation Enduring Freedom, the B-2 flew one of its longest missions to date from Whiteman to Afghanistan and back. The B-2 completed its first-ever combat deployment in

---

[76] Information in this section comes from the U.S. Air Force Fact Sheet for the B-2 Spirit, April 23, 2010, http://www.af.mil/information/factsheets/factsheet.asp?fsID=82.

support of Operation Iraqi Freedom, flying 22 sorties from a forward operating location as well as 27 sorties from Whiteman AFB and releasing more than 1.5 million pounds of munitions. The aircraft received full operational capability status in December 2003. On February 1, 2009, the Air Force's newest command, Air Force Global Strike Command, assumed responsibility for the B-2 from Air Combat Command.

The prime contractor, responsible for overall system design and integration, is Northrop Grumman Integrated Systems Sector. Boeing Military Airplanes Co., Hughes Radar Systems Group, General Electric Aircraft Engine Group, and Vought Aircraft Industries, Inc., are key members of the aircraft contractor team.

General Characteristics
Primary function: Multi-role heavy bomber
Contractor: Northrop Grumman Corp. and **Contractor Team:** Boeing Military Airplanes Co., Hughes Radar Systems Group, General Electric Aircraft Engine Group, and Vought Aircraft Industries, Inc.
Power Plant: Four General Electric F118-GE-100 engines
Thrust: 17,300 pounds each engine
Wingspan: 172 feet (52.12 meters)
Length: 69 feet (20.9 meters)
Height: 17 feet (5.1 meters
Weight: 160,000 pounds (72,575 kilograms)
Maximum Takeoff Weight: 336,500 pounds (152,634 kilograms)
Fuel Capacity: 167,000 pounds (75750 kilograms)
Payload: 40,000 pounds (18,144 kilograms)
Speed: High subsonic
Range: Intercontinental
Ceiling: 50,000 feet (15,240 meters)
Armament: Conventional or nuclear weapons
Crew: Two pilots
Unit cost: Approximately $1.157 billion (fiscal 98 constant dollars)
Initial operating capability: April 1997
Inventory: Active force: 20 (1 test); ANG: 0; Reserve: 0

Appendix B. Plans for B-52H Bomber Sustainment and Modernization

B-52H Master Plan and Requirements[77]

The *B-5H2 Bomber Master Plan* outlines Air Force Global Strike Command's (AFGSC's) plans, programs, requirements, and strategic vision for the B-52 platform to meet the nation's airborne strategic nuclear deterrence and global precision attack mission objectives. Near-term modernization and sustainment efforts are identified for the time period 2012 to 2018. Far-term modernization and sustainment efforts are identified as those required in the 2019 to 2032 time period. AFGSC Director of Plans, Programs and Requirements (HQ AFGSC A5/8) is responsible for producing and updating the master plan.

Assumptions

The B-52H Bomber Master Plan is based on the following assumptions:

- The B-52H will conduct its assigned nuclear mission through 2040.

- The B-52H will continue to conduct its assigned conventional mission through 2040.

- The B-52H fleet size will consist of not more than 76 airframes through 2040.

- Conversion of a required number of B-52Hs to a conventional-only role by 2018 for New START compliance.

- The current B-52H service life goal is 2040.

- There will be no change to current B-52H basing.

- Unfunded risks and issues require prioritization and validation through the resource allocation and POM (program objectives memorandum) process.

- The nuclear enterprise will continue to be a top priority for the Air Force and the primary mission of Air Force Global Strike Command.

Current B-52H Sustainment and Modernization Efforts

The following is a summary of B-52H sustainment and modernization initiatives currently in the program of record (POR) that are either just being completed or are currently in progress. (Asterisks denote sustainment and modernization efforts that could be considered essential to the B-52H's ability to operate in A2/AD threat environments.)

> *** Combat Network Communications Technology (CONECT):** The B-52 CONECT acquisition program supports nuclear and conventional operations by upgrading the B-52

---

[77] Information in **Appendix B** is from Air Force Global Strike Command's, *B-52 Bomber Master Plan*, June 2012.

fleet with tactical datalink and voice communications capability along with improved threat and situational awareness to support participation in network centric operations.

* Military-Standard-1760 Modernization: Improves the B-52's conventional warfare capability with additional MIL-STD-1760 smart weapons and improved weapons carriage and fully integrates advanced targeting pods with the B-52's offensive avionics system.

B-52 Trainer Upgrades: Includes modernization upgrades to B-52 training devices to support aircrew and maintenance training with the latest B-52 capabilities. Upgrades and modernizations under this program ensure weapons system trainers (simulators) are current with ongoing B-52 modifications.

Arms Control: Arms control activities under the New START create the need to modify a number of B-52s to a conventional only role by removing the aircraft's nuclear Code Enable Switch and associated equipment. This effort requires a complete design to remove the equipment from the aircraft and install metal plates prohibiting reinstallation of removed equipment to comply with treaty protocols.

* Mode S/5 Identification Friend or Foe (IFF): The Mode S/5 program replaces the B-52's aging APX-64 IFF transponder with a modern APX-119 transponder. Mode S/5 IFF is required for flight by the Federal Aviation Administration (FAA), International Civil Aviation Organization (ICAO), and the DOD.

Low Cost Modifications: Miscellaneous, low-cost modernization efforts that stem from the operation and maintenance of a 50-plus-year-old aircraft, such as parts obsolescence, diminishing manufacturing resources, and emerging requirements to add or maintain the existing B-52 capabilities.

B-52 Anti-Skid Replacement: The B-52 anti-skid system is used to maintain control of the aircraft during landing and taxi operations by preventing aircraft skidding. This modification replaces the current anti-skid system with an updated system that resolves obsolescence issues. If not upgraded, the unsupportability of the current anti-skid system is projected to affect aircraft availability starting in 2015.

* B-52 Modernization Research Development Test and Evaluation Efforts: B-52 modernization RDT&E efforts is a comprehensive program to ensure the B-52's ability to perform current and future wartime missions. It includes upgrades to data links, navigation, sensors, weapons, and electronic warfare and training capabilities.

* 1760 Internal Weapons Bay Upgrade (IWBU): The 1760 IWBU modification allows the B-52 to carry J-series weapons such as the Joint Direct Attack Munitions (JDAM), Joint Air-to-Surface Standoff Missile (JASSM), JASSM-ER (extended range), and Miniature Air Launched Decoy (MALD) weapons in the B-52's internal weapons bay.

Future B-52H Sustainment and Modernization Requirements

While the current B-52H weapon system is capable of meeting today's strategic deterrence and conventional taskings, it may require continued sustainment and modernization efforts to remain airworthy and viable against 21st century A2/AD threats. For the B-52H to continue meeting mission requirements, Air Force Global Strike Command recommends considering the following modernization and sustainment efforts for future appropriations consideration. These efforts are organized into five broad categories: airframe, avionics, communications systems, weapons interfaces, and supporting infrastructure. A detailed explanation of each category's specific recommendations can be found in the B-52H's Master Plan.

Airframe: The airframe is comprised of structural components, engines, flight controls, and miscellaneous mechanical systems. Several B-52 airframe subsystems such as the existing B-52 analog Yaw Electronic Control Unit/Pitch Electronic Control Unit and the Anti-Skid Control Unit within the Anti-Skid System are becoming unsupportable due to parts obsolescence, lack of test equipment, specialized tools, troubleshooting guides, and experienced repair personnel. Continued full funding for these programs could mitigate these problems.

Avionics Systems: Avionics systems are comprised of defensive systems, offensive systems, and navigation systems. Several avionics subsystems are suffering from obsolescence and supportability issues. For example, the current radar antenna was never upgraded, uses 1950s technology and is projected to become unsupportable in the near future. In addition, the Electronic Warfare (EW) suite is experiencing parts obsolescence, diminishing manufacturing sources, and ineffectiveness against the technologically advancing A2/AD threats.

Communications Systems: Communications systems are comprised of cryptographic, tactical, emergency, and survivable subsystems. The biggest near-term communications concern involves the family of advanced beyond line-of-sight terminals. Delays in the program are putting the Extremely High-Frequency (EHF) program at risk by not meeting U.S. Strategic Command's (USSTRATCOM) need dates based on projected Military Strategic and Tactical Relay Satellite (MILSTAR) Ultra High Frequency Satellite Communications (UHF SATCOM) end-of-life projections. Further delays will impact the B-52's ability to receive Emergency Action Messages (EAMs) and Report-Backs in support of USSTRATCOM's nuclear command and control requirements.

Longer-term communications concerns involve the integration of an advanced tactical datalink and an advanced secure, broadband, beyond line-of-sight datalink for continuous, survivable command and control coordination, and improved reception of weapons retargeting data and mission updates.

Weapons Interfaces: Weapons interfaces are systems designed to support, carry, communicate with and/or launch weapons from the B-52. Near-term needs include the integration of an Advanced Targeting Pod, on-going Military-Standard-1760 internal weapons bay upgrades, integrated weapons interface unit (IWIU) integration on external weapons pylons, and a GPS interface unit/programmable keyboard upgrade to the offensive avionics system.

Supporting Infrastructure: B-52 supporting infrastructure includes trainers, simulators, test equipment, aircraft ground equipment, and weapon system testing that support the B-52 platform.

Figure B-1. Graphical Summary of B-52 Sustainment and Modernization Master Plan

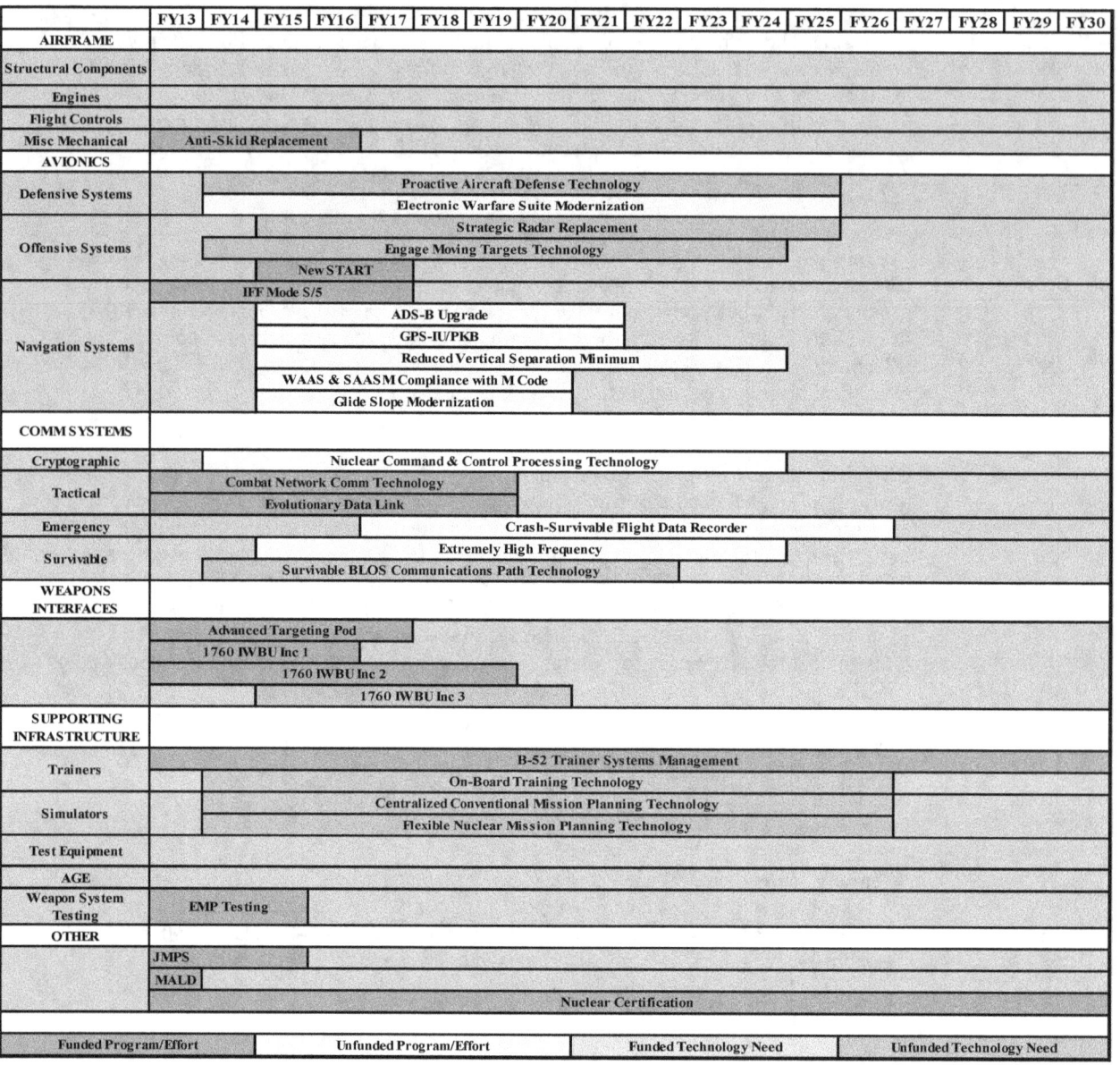

Source: Air Force Global Strike Command, B-52 Bomber Master Plan, June 2012, p. 10.

Figure B-2. Historical Comparison of B-52 Appropriated Funding and the Average Annual Mission Capable (MC) Rates for the B-52 Fleet

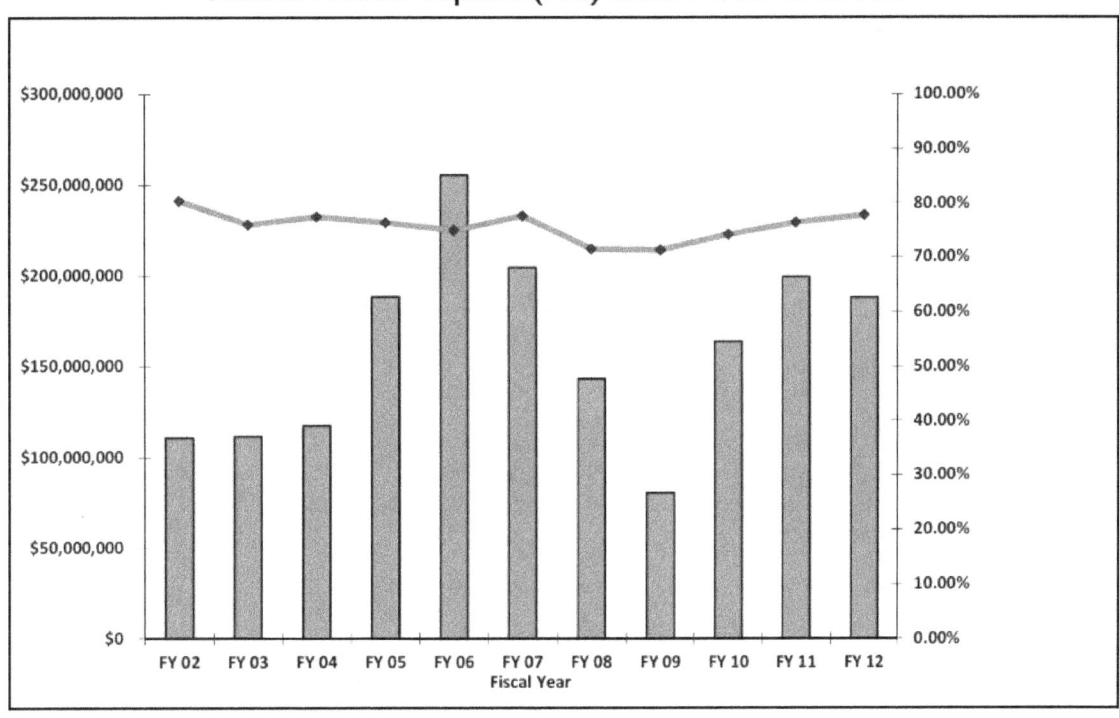

Source: National Defense Authorization Acts, Appropriation Acts, and Committee Reports for Fiscal Years 2002 to 2012 and mission capable rates as reported to Headquarters U.S. Air Force by Global Strike Command.

Note: Mission capable rate is defined as the percentage of aircraft in the fleet that are capable of performing its intended wartime mission.

Appendix C. Plans for B-1 Bomber Sustainment and Modernization

B-1 Strategic Action and Investment Plan (SAIP)[78]

Similar to the B-52H and B-2's Master Plans, the B-1 sustainment and modernization plan is captured in the *B-1 Strategic Action and Investment Plan (SAIP)*. B-1 requirements are managed by Air Combat Command's (ACC's) B-1 Aircraft Branch (ACC/A8A1) within the ACC/A8A Combat Aircraft Division. In 2011, the B-1 Aircraft Branch contracted with the consulting firm of Whitney, Bradley & Brown, Inc. to research, study, and develop a cost optimized and time phased B-1 sustainment and modernization plan. The resulting B-1 SAIP provides detailed analysis and recommendations for the period 2014 to 2025 and presents optimum B-1 portfolios of sustainment and modernization efforts for the FY14, FY16, and FY18 Programs Objective Memorandum (POM). The results of this effort produced three sustainment and modernization plans designed to maximize the benefit to be received from three, assumed funding levels dependent on Air Force requested and congressionally provided appropriations.

- Appropriation of $179 million per year (out to 2022) should complete existing sustainment and modernization programs and fund only those sustainment programs needed to maintain existing B-1 capabilities. The B-1 SAIP concludes that $179 million represents the minimum feasible B-1 modernization and sustainment funding level.

- The B-1 SAIP concluded that appropriations of $250 million per year (out to 2022) is the minimum recommended funding level for B-1 sustainment and modernization. At this level, several high benefit capabilities could be funded, which would reduce Air Force ownership costs and potentially increase the B-1's operational effectiveness.

- Appropriations of $400 million per year is the highest considered funding profile recommended by the B-1 SAIP and would be sufficient to fund most of the recommended B-1 sustainment and modernization efforts out to 2022.

The B-1 SAIP concludes that the Air Force should request at least $250 million per year for B-1 sustainment and modernization. Appropriations at this level and above are anticipated to provide near-term solutions to weapon system capability gaps and shortfalls while ensuring the B-1 is capable of supporting national security objectives.

Assumptions

The B-1 Bomber Strategic Action and Investment Plan (SAIP) is based on the following assumptions:

- There will be a continued requirement to strike fleeting or time sensitive targets.

---

[78] Information in **Appendix C** is from Air Force Air Combat Command's, *B-1 Strategic Action and Investment Plan (SAIP)*, May 10, 2012.

- The overall force structure within the Air Force will continue to be reduced, emphasizing the need for availability of existing platforms such as the B-1.

- B-1 force structure will remain steady over the SAIP timeline.

- B-1s may be employed from the continental United States or applicable forward-deployed locations, as warranted by the scenario and theater requirements.

- Budget pressures dictate that B-1 aircraft be sustained in the most affordable manner possible.

- Reductions in manpower will continue to highlight the need for efficiencies.

- Irregular Warfare operations will continue throughout the service life of the B-1.

Current B-1 Sustainment and Modernization Efforts

The following is a summary of the major B-1 sustainment and modernization initiatives that are currently in the program of record (POR) that are either just completing or are currently in progress. The costs of these PORs were factored into the SAIP's sustainment and modernization funding analysis and are reflected in the three assumed funding levels. (Asterisks denote sustainment and modernization efforts that could be considered essential to the B-1's ability to operate in A2/AD threat environments.)

* **Fully Integrated Data Link:** FIDL will provide the B-1 with Link-16 line-of-sight (LOS) and Joint Range Extension (JRE) beyond-line-of-sight (BLOS) data link capability and supports machine-to-machine transfer of targeting data to the B-1's weapons control computers.

Simulator Digital Control Loading: Simulator digital control loading is a modification to the B-1's Weapon System Trainer(s) (WSTs) that will replace the existing hydraulically-operated control loading system with a digital control loading system. Control loading provides force feedback for the pilot's flight control stick and pedals; the WST flight stations are unusable without a working control loading system. The existing system faces obsolescence and diminishing manufacturing sources (DMS) issues, with some critical parts having no spares.

Central Integrated Test System: CITS is the B-1's fault diagnostic and fault isolation system. The current CITS processor is at maximum memory/throughput, thus inhibiting fault detection and isolation for current systems and future B-1 upgrades. This modification provides a new processor, upgraded displays, and new software that will enhance diagnostic capabilities, improve aircraft turnaround time, and reduce maintenance costs. This program will also alleviate the current diminishing manufacturing source issue with this system.

* **Inertial Navigation System Replacement:** Provides for the replacement of a line replaceable unit (LRU) in the B-1's inertial navigation system. The B-1 INS provides autonomous capability to navigate globally, without the aid of ground-based and global positioning system navigation aids, as well as engage ground targets with a high level of precision. The current INS system is plagued with severe diminishing manufacturing source issues.

* **Radar Improvement Upgrade:** The B-1B Radar Reliability and Maintainability Improvement Program (RMIP) consists of the replacement of two high-failure-rate radar Line Replaceable Units (LRUs) and the supporting software conversion of legacy radar modes. The Radar RMIP is intended to provide B-1B combat forces with an updated

offensive radar system that should improve mission capable (MC) rates and eliminate issues with diminishing manufacturing sources (DMS).

* Visual Situation Display Upgrade: The Vertical Situation Display Upgrade (VSDU) is a safety-critical program that replaces the B-1's pilot and co-pilot primary flight displays and associated flight instruments. The current VSDs are monochrome cathode ray tube displays and "steam gauge" primary flight instruments which are experiencing severe diminishing manufacturing source issues with the potential to ground the aircraft. Spares are no longer procurable due to obsolescence. VSDU installs two 8" x 6" color displays at the pilot and co-pilot stations to provide primary flight information and backups to meet flight safety standards.

Self-Contained Attitude Indicator: The SCAI is a backup to the B-1's primary flight instruments and provides pilots with indications of aircraft attitude, airspeed, Mach, altitude and vertical velocity. This development effort will replace the current obsolete legacy SCAI with a more reliable and supportable off-the-shelf display.

Gyro Stabilization System Replacement (GSSR): This program is procuring and installing line replaceable units (LRUs) in the B-1's GSS, which is part of the aircraft's navigation system. This modification provides for replacement of the high maintenance/high cost/high failure rate GSS LRUs with high reliability LRUs.

B-1 Training Support: This effort modifies and replaces computer components in the B-1 aircraft Maintenance Training Devices (MTDs). These MTDs are currently running on computer systems from the late 1990s and are using nearly 100% of the computer resources available to them. As such, no excess computer capacity exists to support current updates, including current B-1 modification efforts. This modification will update the hardware with modern Commercial Off-The-Shelf (COTS) computer systems and will re-host the software on the new hardware, allowing these MTDs to accept new upgrades and remain concurrent with B-1 upgrades.

* Digital Communications: The digital communications upgrade provides for replacement of a currently installed Ultra High Frequency (UHF) Satellite Communications (SATCOM) beyond line of sight datalink radio system with a Demand Assigned Multiple Access (DAMA) compliant, UHF SATCOM radio. The current system, a temporary modification, was installed in 2002 to support combat operations in Southwest Asia. The current system is not DAMA compliant, which severely limits accessibility to SATCOM channels. In addition, the current system utilizes a system unique datalink, which is not interoperable with standard, joint UHF SATCOM systems.

* B-1 Link 16 Cryptographic Materials: Assistant Secretary of Defense for Command, Control and Communications (ASD/C3I) directed implementation of the DOD Cryptographic Modernization Initiative (CMI) on 23 February 2001.[79] CJCS Notice 6510/NSA 3-9 directs the modernization of all cryptography in military systems in the US, NATO and Coalition nations. To prevent information compromise, the National Security Agency mandate requires Link 16 cryptographic systems to be upgraded.

---

[79] The cryptographic modernization program is a DOD directed, National Security Agency (NSA) Information Assurance Directorate led effort to transform and modernize all cryptography in military command and control, communications, computer, intelligence, surveillance and reconnaissance, information technology, and weapon systems. The program is a multi-billion dollar, multi-year undertaking that will transform cryptographic security capabilities for national security systems at all echelons and points of use.

* **Laptop Controlled Targeting Pod:** LCTP provides advanced targeting pod control, display, and information to all B-1 crewmembers. It allows aircrew to derive precision coordinates for GPS guided weapons, guide laser-guided weapons, and allows aircrew to conduct inflight re-planning of long-range standoff weapons. This effort permanently installs three rack mounted computers and removes temporary targeting pod laptops.

Low Cost Mods: These modifications are low cost B-1 upgrades that address safety, reliability, maintainability, and/or improved system performance issues on the aircraft, support equipment, and simulators/trainers. These funds are required for mission essential B-1 low cost modifications to ensure readiness and B-1 operational requirements.

* **Miscellaneous B-1 Modernization Research, Development, Test and Evaluation Efforts:** This program provides RDT&E funding for the B-1 modernization program. The modernization program addresses potential aircraft obsolescent issues due to diminishing manufacturing sources (DMS) and provides new and improved capabilities to the B-1 weapon system that require significant hardware and software development and testing.

Future B-1 Sustainment and Modernization Requirements

Optimal $250M /Year B-1 Modernization and Sustainment Funding Scenario

Figure C-1 depicts the $250 million/year funding scenario for current programs of record (POR) and the recommended future B-1 modernization and sustainment requirements. $250 million/year is the minimum funding level recommended by the B-1 SAIP where 32, high-benefit capabilities could be funded that could reduce Air Force ownership costs and potentially increase the B-1's operational effectiveness. Authors of the B-1 SAIP believe the 32, high-benefit capabilities represent the optimal combination of future modernization and sustainment needs that could provide the highest benefit at the $250 million/year funding level and is a point of departure when considering other funding levels and future requirements. A detailed description of each of the 32 capabilities can be found in the B-1 SAIP.

Figure C-1. B-1 Strategic Action and Investment Plan, $250 Million/Fiscal Year Funding Scenario

(in millions of dollars)

B-1 Strategic Action and Investment Plan - $250M Funding Scenario									
Modernization Program	FY14 FYDP				FY16 FYDP			FY18 FYDP	Total Program Cost
	2014	2015	2016	2017	2018	2019	2020	2021	2022	
16 Carry					36.2	46.6	21.7	22.0	30.0	156.5
2 Color Flare					3.0	5.0	5.0	5.0	5.0	23.0
ABS CMS			2.0	6.0						8.0
AESA Inc I&II						9.6	53.8	92.5	139.3	295.2
ALE-50 Tester	1.3	1.2	1.4	1.6	1.3					6.8
ARTS	2.4	23.5	28.5	20.8	3.4					78.6
Auto Wire Test Set	1.4									1.4
Bleed Air Blowers					0.5	1.0	0.6	0.6	0.6	3.3
Def Sys Upgrade			20.0	80.0	50.0	45.0	50.0	50.0		295.0
DR-200	6.9	6.9	5.2	5.2						24.2
EMUX Upgrade							26.0	19.0	11.7	56.7
ETCS	0.7	1.7	2.7	3.3	3.3	3.3				15.0
ETU	15.0	12.0	17.0	2.4	11.2					57.6
FCGMS Upgrade							21.0	16.0	11.7	48.7
FCGMS Wiring		7.0	5.0	5.2	5.2	5.2	5.2	5.2		38.0
Hydro Titanium			0.5	1.0	2.0	2.0	2.0	2.0		9.5
ISIS					15.0	11.0	9.1	9.1	5.2	49.4
ITPaC	18.5	25.7	7.0	7.0						58.2
JSOW B III							5.0	10.0	10.0	25.0
LRASM-A	8.0	10.0								18.0
MALD-J					10.0	25.0	38.0	4.0	4.0	81.0
Maritime Int Wpn					0.8	0.8				1.6
MLG					1.5	0.6	0.6	0.6	0.5	3.8
P5 ADL					3.0	7.0	2.0	2.0		14.0
Current PORs	173.6	142.4	146.2	104.5	56.6					623.3
R/EW Test Equip	1.0									1.0
Rdr Altimeter					4.4	14.5	4.8	4.4	4.4	32.5
SCDU					0.5	1.5	2.0	2.0	2.0	8.0
SDB				10.0	40.0	50.0				100.0
Sim for IBS	10.4	14.3	12.0	0.7	0.7					38.1
Weapon Data Link (WDL)									23.0	23.0
WST DCLS	3.0	3.2	3.3							9.5
Total/FY	242.2	247.9	250.8	247.7	248.6	228.1	246.8	244.4	247.4	2203.9

Source: B-1 Strategic Action and Investment Plan (SAIP), May 10, 2012.

Figure C-2. Historical Comparison of B-1 Appropriated Funding and the Average Annual Mission Capable (MC) Rates for the B-1 fleet

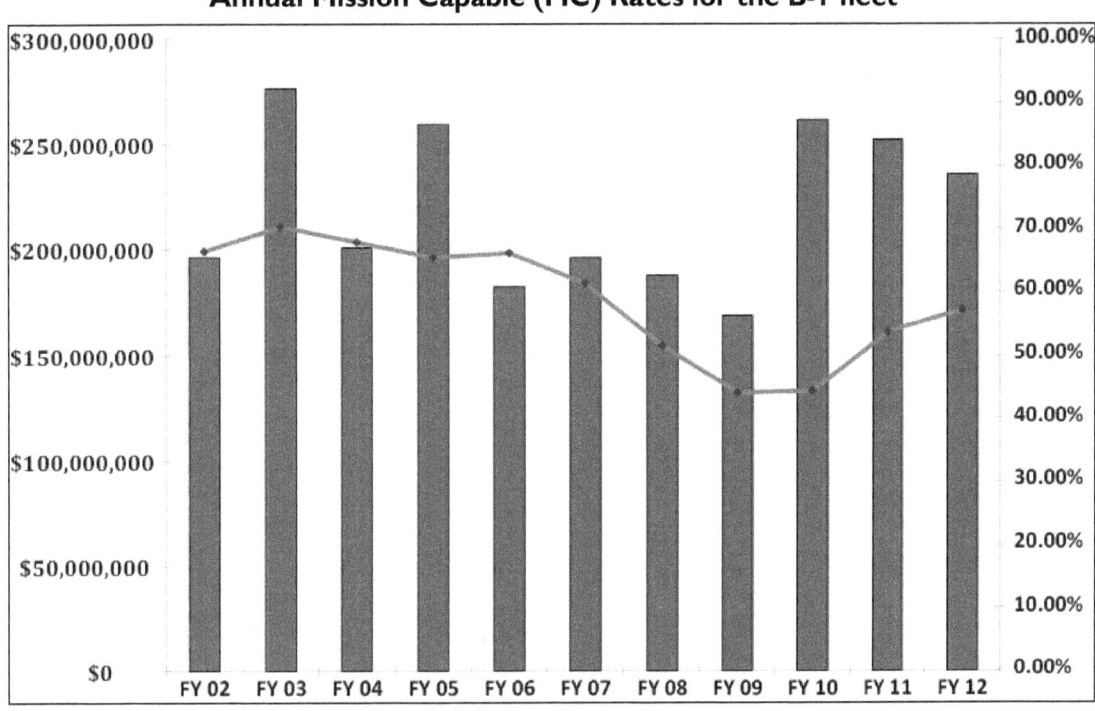

Source: National Defense Authorization Acts, Appropriation Acts, and Committee Reports for Fiscal Years 2002 to 2012 and mission capable rates as reported to Headquarters U.S. Air Force by Air Combat Command.

Note: Mission capable rate is defined as the percentage of aircraft in the fleet that are capable of performing its intended wartime mission.

Appendix D. Plans for B-2 Sustainment and Modernization

B-2 Master Plan and Requirements[80]

The *B-2 Bomber Master Plan* outlines Air Force Global Strike Command's (AFGSC's) plans, programs, requirements, and strategic vision for the B-2 platform to meet the nation's airborne strategic nuclear deterrence and global precision attack mission needs. Near-term modernization and sustainment efforts are identified for the time period 2012 to 2018. Far-term modernization and sustainment efforts are identified as those required in the 2019 to 2032 time period. AFGSC Director of Plans, Programs and Requirements (HQ AFGSC A5/8) is responsible for producing and updating the master plan.

Assumptions

The B-2 Bomber Master Plan is based on the following assumptions:

- The B-2 will continue to conduct currently assigned nuclear and conventional missions well into the 2050s.

- The B-2 fleet size will remain at 20 aircraft through 2058.

- The B-2 planned end-of-life will remain 2058.

- There will be no change to current B-2 basing.

- Unfunded risks and issues require prioritization and validation through the resource allocation and program objective memorandum (POM) process.

- The B-2 will continue to be required to penetrate and employ weapons in highly defended anti-access/area denial environments well into 2050.

- The B-2 will continue to be a primary component in the USAF Long Range Strike (LRS) family of systems.

- The B-2 will incorporate all new, applicable air-to-ground weapons including the new cruise missile and the ability to employ weapons to defeat and destroy hardened and deeply buried targets.

- The B-52 will incorporate beyond-line-of-sight (BLOS) connectivity for conventional, as well as nuclear taskings [survivable, assured nuclear command and control].

- Air Force Global Strike Command and Air Combat Command will continue to work cooperatively on B-2 requirements in accordance with applicable Memoranda of Agreement.

---

[80] Information **Appendix D** is from Air Force Global Strike Command's, B-2 Bomber Master Plan, June 2012.

Current B-2 Sustainment and Modernization Efforts

The following is a summary of B-2 sustainment and modernization initiatives currently in the program of record (POR) that are either just completing or are currently in progress. (Asterisks denote sustainment and modernization efforts that could be considered essential to the B-2's ability to operate in A2/AD threat environments.)

* **Extremely High Frequency Satellite Communications (EHF SATCOM) and Computer Upgrade Program:** The aging Ultra High Frequency (UHF) Military Satellite Communications system is being phased out and replaced by the Advanced Extremely High Frequency (AEHF) Satellite Communications (SATCOM) system. The B-2 Extremely High Frequency (EHF) SATCOM program supports the replacement of the B-2's UHF Terminal Set with an EHF SATCOM system that will be compatible with the legacy MILSTAR I/II satellite constellation and the future AEHF satellite constellation.

* **Massive Ordnance Penetrator Integration:** The B-2 is the only anti-access penetrating platform capable of delivering the Massive Ordnance Penetrator (MOP) against hardened, deeply buried targets. Integration of the 30,000 lb class MOP provides the ability to hold additional hardened, deeply buried targets at risk beyond those achievable with current munitions. The MOP integration program will design, develop, integrate, and test hardware and software required for carriage, jettison, and release of MOP from the B-2.

* **Low Observable Signature and Supportability Modifications (LOSSM) Diagnostics:** LOSSM diagnostics equipment projects help reduce low observable (LO) maintenance, increase aircraft availability and improves the combat ready LO signature for the B-2 fleet.

B-2 Trainer System Upgrade: Trainer system upgrades keep the B-2 family of trainers current with aircraft system updates while countering equipment obsolescence issues. Enhancements are provided to the B-2 family of trainers to include the Weapon System Trainers, Mission Trainer, Cockpit Procedures Trainers, Computerized Maintenance Training System, Weapon System Training Aids, Weapons Load Trainer, Crew Escape System Maintenance Trainer, Flight Control System Trainer, instructor-operator station, and Training System Support Center.

* **Link-16/Center Instrument Display/In-Flight Replanner (CID/IFR):** Link-16 CID/IFR allows the B-2 access to theater tactical data links, improving on-board situational awareness while greatly enhancing the ability of theater commanders to coordinate the B-2 with other assets. The Center Instrument Display Digital Video Recorder provides the ability to record video signals from the display to the existing recorders in the cockpit. This capability allows mission playback, operational assessments and de-briefs, and provides aircrew training.

Radar Modernization Program (RMP): Completed in the third quarter FY12, this program brought all operational and flight test B-2 aircraft radars into frequency compliance.

* **Low Observable Signature and Supportability Modifications (LOSSM) Program Structures/Materials:** This program implements a mix of over 20 improvements to the B-2's low observable (LO) support equipment, structures, and materials designed to slow signature degradation and to improve LO supportability. LOSSM projects decrease low observable (LO) maintenance, increase aircraft availability, and maintain and improve the combat-ready LO signature for the B-2 fleet.

* **Defensive Management System Modernization (DMS-M):** The DMS-M program addresses capability gaps, obsolescence, and supportability issues associated with the B2's legacy DMS system. DMS-M will upgrade the B-2's self-defense capabilities against

improved, 21st century A2/AD enemy air defenses. DMS-M is the #1 priority modification program in the B-2 program office and will resolve the #1 obsolescence issue in the B-2 fleet.

* Stores Management Operational Flight Program (SMOFP) Re-host and Mixed Carriage Modification: This program will re-host the B-2's stores management operational flight software onto a larger, more capable processor, enabling the B-2 to carry a mixed weapons carriage with a Rotary Launcher Assembly (RLA) in one weapons bay and a Smart Bomb Rack Assembly (SBRA) in the other weapons bay.

* Common Very Low Frequency Receiver (CVR Increment 1): This program provides the B-2 with a survivable, beyond-line-of-sight communication path for receipt of Emergency Action Messages (EAMs) to support United States Strategic Command's (USSTRATCOM) nuclear command and control requirements.

Low Cost Engine Modifications: B-2 engine improvements include the F118 engine service life extension program, the extended mission oil tank upgrade, and stage one and three engine fan blade improvements that will reduce engine changes and increase aircraft availability.

Low Cost Modifications: These modifications are low cost B-2 upgrades that address safety, reliability, maintainability, and/or improved system performance issues on the B-2 aircraft, support equipment, and simulators/trainers. These funds are required for mission essential B-2 low cost modifications to ensure readiness and B-2 operational requirements.

* B-2 Modernization Research, Development, Test and Evaluation efforts: To ensure the B-2 fleet can accomplish its nuclear and conventional mission in highly defended and anti-access environments, periodic modernization efforts must be undertaken to upgrade combat capability as well as improve the viability, supportability, and survivability of the weapon system. RDT&E funding ensures recent and ongoing investments in necessary avionics, structures, communications, and weapons upgrades keep the B-2 viable in the immediate future.

Baseline Support: Baseline Support maintains the B-2 unique flight test aircraft, as well as obtains, modifies, and operates a flying test bed, developmental hardware/software and test equipment, to support developmental systems integration and flight test.

Future B-2 Sustainment and Modernization Requirements

While the current B-2 weapons system is capable of meeting today's strategic deterrence and conventional taskings, it may require continued sustainment and modernization efforts to remain airworthy and viable against 21st century anti-access/areal denial (A2/AD) threats. Consequently, the B-2 will require continued system review and testing, adaptation to emerging technologies and threats, and attention to facilities and ground support equipment in order for the weapon system to remain viable out to the 2050s. The following is a brief summary of Air Force Global Strike Command's recommendations to support the B-2 from 2012 through 2032. The recommendations are designed to address sustainment challenges while ensuring future modernization and acquisition efforts remain integrated and synchronized to meet the B-2's operational requirements. The guidance is organized into three broad categories: airframe, communications systems, and supporting infrastructure. A detailed explanation of each category's specific recommendations can be found in the B-2's Master Plan.

Airframe: The airframe category is comprised of avionics, low-observable, weapons interfaces, flight controls, engines, and miscellaneous mechanical subsystems. Many issues within these systems currently affect viability, availability, and turnaround time of the B-2 weapon system. For example, low-observable maintenance continues to be problematic due to high repair costs, labor-intensive procedures, supportability issues, and degradation of aircraft radar signature. The 1980s era Defensive Management System technology suffers from obsolescence and supportability issues and requires modernization. Mixed weapons carriage flexibility is constrained due to system limitations such as computer processing, memory and throughput. These issues should continue to be addressed as they reduce the B-2's flexibility to deliver desired effects, its ability to penetrate A2/AD threats, and ultimately, its combat survivability.

Communications System: The communications system category is comprised of cryptographic, tactical, emergency and survivable communications subsystems. The cryptographic system requires modernization due to obsolescence and decertification issues leading to security and sustainment concerns. Currently, the aircraft's primary beyond-line-of-sight (BLOS) communications capability is provided via the UHF Military Strategic and Tactical Relay Satellite (MILSTAR) system, which has already exceeded its design life and is nearing life expected end-of-life.

Supporting Infrastructure: The supporting infrastructure category includes—but is not limited to—depot , trainers, simulators, test equipment, aerospace ground equipment (AGE), flight testing, and software that support the B-2 weapon system. Test and support equipment are aging and beginning to suffer from design life, supportability, and parts obsolescence issues.

Figure D-1. Graphical Summary of B-2 Sustainment and Modernization Master Plan

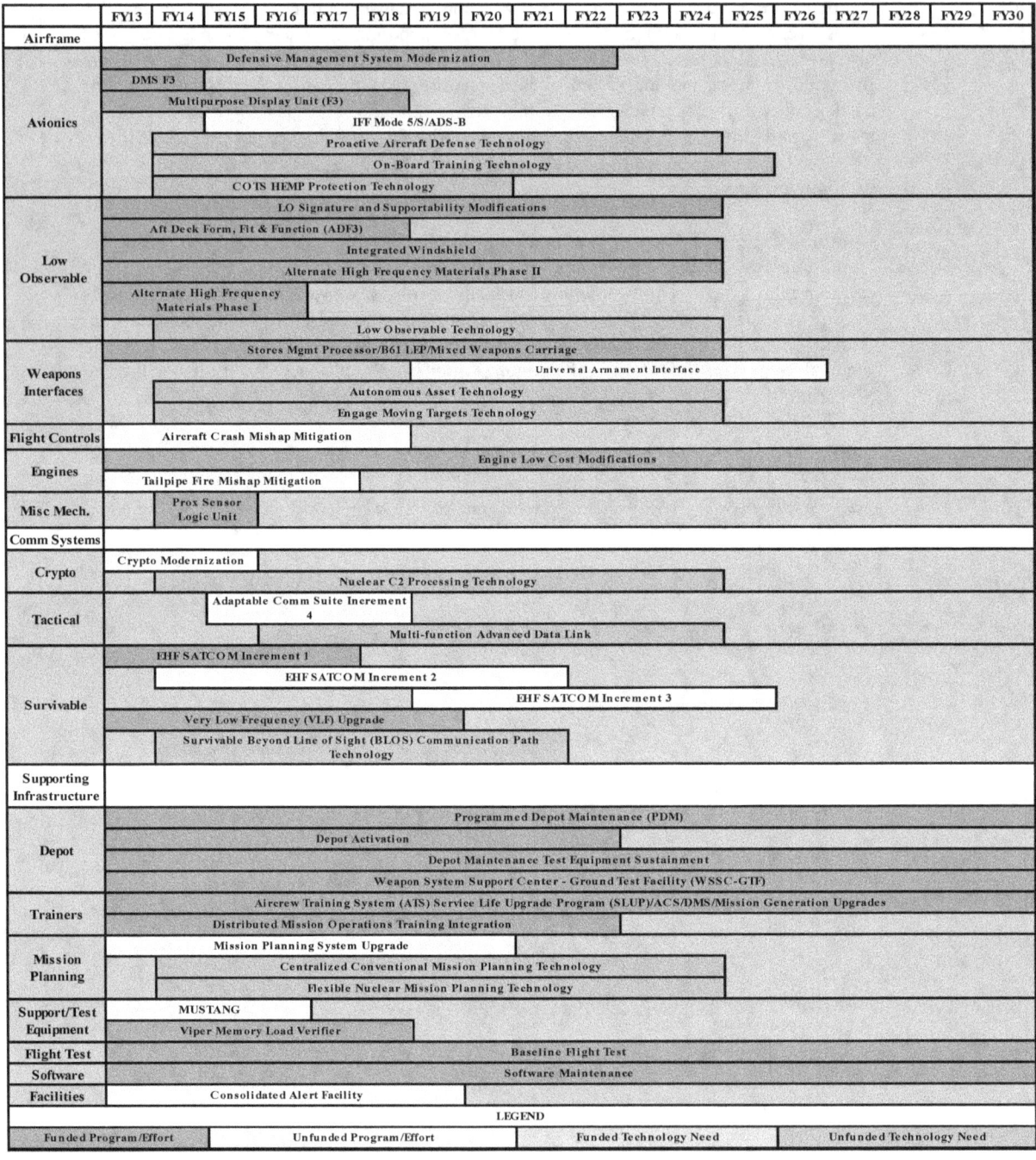

Source: Air Force Global Strike Command, B-2 Bomber Master Plan, June 2012, p 10.

Congressional Research Service   62

Figure D-2. Historical Comparison of B-2 Appropriated Funding and the Average Annual Mission Capable (MC) Rates for the B-2 fleet

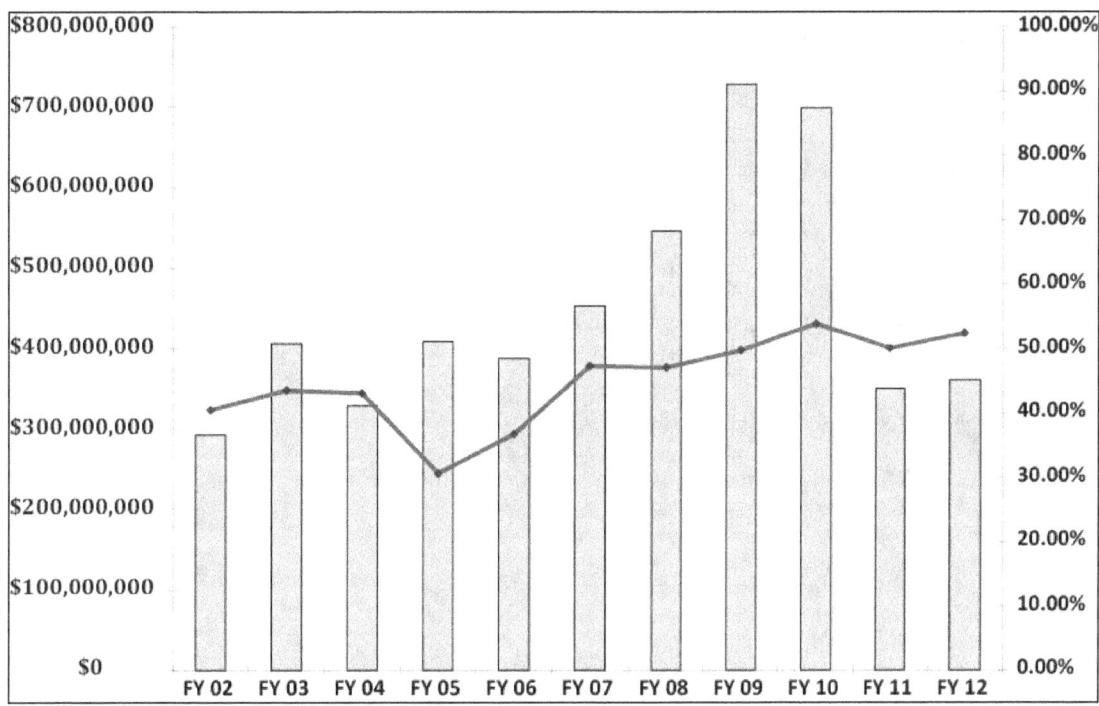

Source: National Defense Authorization Acts, Appropriation Acts, and Committee Reports for Fiscal Years 2002 to 2012 and mission capable rates as reported to Headquarters U.S. Air Force by Global Strike Command.

Note: Mission capable rate is defined as the percentage of aircraft in the fleet that are capable of performing its intended wartime mission.

Appendix E. Legislative Activity FY2011-FY2013

FY2011 National Defense Authorization Act (P.L. 111-383)

TITLE 1 - Procurement

Subtitle C - Joint and Multiservice Matters

SEC. 126. INTEGRATION OF SOLID STATE LASER SYSTEMS INTO CERTAIN AIRCRAFT.

(a) ANALYSIS OF FEASIBILITY REQUIRED.—The Secretary of Defense shall conduct an analysis of the feasibility of integrating solid state laser systems into the aircraft platforms specified in subsection (b) for purposes of permitting such aircraft to accomplish their missions, including to provide close air support.

(b) AIRCRAFT—The aircraft platforms specified in this subsection shall include, at a minimum, the following:

(1) The C–130 aircraft.

(2) The B–1 bomber aircraft.

(3) The F–35 fighter aircraft.

(c) SCOPE OF ANALYSIS.—The analysis required by subsection (a) shall include a determination of the following:

(1) The estimated cost per unit of each laser system analyzed.

(2) The estimated cost of operation and maintenance of each aircraft platform specified in subsection (b) in connection with each laser system analyzed, noting that the fidelity of such analysis may not be uniform for all aircraft platforms.

TITLE X - General Provisions

Subtitle F - Studies and Reports

SEC. 1056. REQUIRED REPORTS CONCERNING BOMBER MODERNIZATION, SUSTAINMENT, AND RECAPITALIZATION EFFORTS IN SUPPORT OF THE NATIONAL DEFENSE STRATEGY.

(a) AIR FORCE REPORT.—

(1) REPORT REQUIRED.—Not later than 360 days after the date of the enactment of this Act, the Secretary of the Air Force shall submit to the congressional defense committees a report that includes—

(A) a discussion of the cost, schedule, and performance of all planned efforts to modernize and keep viable the existing B–1, B–2, and B–52 bomber fleets and a discussion of the forecasted service-life and all sustainment challenges that the

Secretary of the Air Force may confront in keeping those platforms viable until the anticipated retirement of such aircraft;

(B) a discussion, presented in a comparison and contrast type format, of the scope of the 2007 Next-Generation Long Range Strike Analysis of Alternatives guidance and subsequent Analysis of Alternatives report tasked by the Under Secretary of Defense for Acquisition, Technology, and Logistics in the September 11, 2006, Acquisition Decision Memorandum, as compared to the scope and directed guidance of the year 2010 Long Range Strike Study effort currently being conducted by the Under Secretary of Defense for Policy and the Office of the Secretary of Defense's Cost Assessment and Program Evaluation Office; and

(C) a discussion of the preliminary costs, any development, testing, fielding and operational employment challenges, capability gaps, limitations, and shortfalls of the Secretary of Defense's plan to field a long-range, penetrating, survivable, persistent and enduring "family of systems" as compared to the preliminary costs, any development, testing, fielding, and operational employment of a singular platform that encompasses all the required aforementioned characteristics.

(2) PREPARATION OF REPORT.—The report under paragraph (1) shall be prepared by a federally funded research and development center selected by the Secretary of the Air Force and submitted to the Secretary for submittal by the Secretary in accordance with that paragraph.

(b) COST ANALYSIS AND PROGRAM EVALUATION REPORT.—Not later than 180 days after the date of the enactment of this Act, the Director of the Cost Analysis and Program Evaluation of the Office of the Secretary of Defense shall submit to the congressional defense committees a report that includes—

(1) the assumptions and estimated life-cycle costs of the Department's long-range, penetrating, survivable, persistent, and enduring "family of systems" platforms; and

(2) the assumptions and estimated life-cycle costs of the Next Generation Platform program, as planned, prior to the cancellation of the program on April 6, 2009.

TITLE XII - Matters Relating to Foreign Nations

Subtitle C - Reports and Other Matters

SEC. 1238. REPORT ON UNITED STATES EFFORTS TO DEFEND AGAINST THREATS POSED BY THE ANTI-ACCESS AND AREA-DENIAL CAPABILITIES OF CERTAIN NATION-STATES.

(a) FINDING.—Congress finds that the 2010 report on the Department of Defense Quadrennial Defense Review concludes that "[a]nti-access strategies seek to deny outside countries the ability to project power into a region, thereby allowing aggression or other destabilizing actions to be conducted by the anti-access power. Without dominant capabilities to project power, the integrity of United States alliances and security partnerships could be called into question, reducing United States security and influence and increasing the possibility of conflict".

(b) SENSE OF CONGRESS.—It is the sense of Congress that, in light of the finding in subsection (a), the Secretary of Defense should ensure that the United States has the appropriate authorities, capabilities, and force structure to defend against any potential future threats posed by the anti-access and area-denial capabilities of potentially hostile foreign countries.

(c) REPORT.—Not later than April 1, 2011, the Secretary of Defense shall submit to the Committees on Armed Services of the Senate and the House of Representatives a report on United States efforts to defend against any potential future threats posed by the anti-access and area-denial capabilities of potentially hostile nation-states.

(d) ELEMENTS.—The report required under subsection (c) shall include the following:

(1) An assessment of any potential future threats posed by the anti-access and area-denial capabilities of potentially hostile foreign countries, including an identification of the foreign countries with such capabilities, the nature of such capabilities, and the possible advances in such capabilities over the next 10 years.

(2) A description of any efforts by the Department of Defense to address the potential future threats posed by the anti-access and area-denial capabilities of potentially hostile foreign countries.

(3) A description of the authorities, capabilities, and force structure that the United States may require over the next 10 years to address the threats posed by the anti-access and area-denial capabilities of potentially hostile foreign countries.

(e) FORM.—The report required under subsection (c) shall be submitted in unclassified form, but may contain a classified annex if necessary.

(f) DEFINITIONS.—In this section—

(1) the term ''anti-access'', with respect to capabilities, means any action that has the effect of slowing the deployment of friendly forces into a theater, preventing such forces from operating from certain locations within that theater, or causing such forces to operate from distances farther from the locus of conflict than such forces would normally prefer; and

(2) the term ''area-denial'', with respect to capabilities, means operations aimed to prevent freedom of action of friendly forces in the more narrow confines of the area under a potentially hostile nation-state's direct control, including actions by an adversary in the air, on land, and on and under the sea to contest and prevent joint operations within a defended battlespace.

FY2012 Department of Defense Appropriations (H.Rept. 112-331 to Accompany H.R. 2055)

Retirement of B-1 Aircraft

The fiscal year 2012 budget request includes a proposal to retire six B–1 bomber aircraft. The conferees understand that the B–1 fleet continues to operate almost constantly over Afghanistan in support of troops on the ground and that the B–1 is a critical component of the Nation's long-range strike capabilities. The Air Force proposed to reinvest less than 40 percent of the savings from aircraft retirements in the B–1 modernization program across the Future Years Defense Program. The conferees are concerned that premature retirement of six B–1 aircraft could negatively impact long-range strike capabilities. Therefore, the conferees direct the Secretary of the Air Force to reinvest a larger portion of savings realized from B–1 aircraft retirements, to the extent authorized by law, in the sustainment and modernization of the B–1 fleet.

FY2012 National Defense Authorization Act (P.L. 112-81)

TITLE I – Procurement

Subtitle D – Air Force Programs

SEC. 132. LIMITATIONS ON USE OF FUNDS TO RETIRE B–1 BOMBER AIRCRAFT.

(a) IN GENERAL.—None of the funds authorized to be appropriated by this Act for fiscal year 2012 for the Department of Defense may be obligated or expended to retire any B–1 bomber aircraft on or before the date on which the Secretary of the Air Force submits to the congressional defense committees the plan described in subsection (b).

(b) PLAN DESCRIBED.—The plan described in this subsection is a plan for retiring B–1 bomber aircraft that includes the following:

(1) An identification of each B–1 bomber aircraft that will be retired and the disposition plan for such aircraft.

(2) An estimate of the savings that will result from the proposed retirement of B–1 bomber aircraft in each calendar year through calendar year 2022.

(3) An estimate of the amount of the savings described in paragraph (2) that will be reinvested in the modernization of B–1 bomber aircraft still in service in each calendar year through calendar year 2022.

(4) A modernization plan for sustaining the remaining B–1 bomber aircraft through at least calendar year 2022.

(5) An estimate of the amount of funding required to fully fund the modernization plan described in paragraph (4) for each calendar year through calendar year 2022.

(c) POST-PLAN B–1 RETIREMENT.—

(1) IN GENERAL.—During the period described by paragraph (4), the Secretary of the Air Force shall maintain in a common capability configuration not less than 36 B–1 aircraft as combat coded aircraft.

(2) FY 2014 AND THEREAFTER.—After the period described in paragraph (4), the Secretary shall maintain not less than—

(A) 35 B–1 aircraft as combat-coded aircraft in a common capability configuration until September 30, 2014;

(B) 34 such aircraft as combat-coded aircraft in a common capability configuration until September 30, 2015; and

(C) 33 such aircraft as combat-coded aircraft in a common capability configuration until September 30, 2016.

(3) TOTAL AMOUNT OF RETIRED B–1 AIRCRAFT.—The Secretary may not retire more than a total of six B–1 aircraft, including the B–1 aircraft retired in accordance with this subsection.

(4) PERIOD DESCRIBED.—The period described in this paragraph is the period beginning on the date on which the plan described in subsection (b) is submitted to the congressional defense committees and ending on September 30, 2013.

(5) COMBAT-CODED AIRCRAFT DEFINED.—In this subsection, the term "combat-coded aircraft" means aircraft assigned to meet the primary aircraft authorization to a unit for the performance of its wartime mission.

SEC. 134. AVAILABILITY OF FISCAL YEAR 2011 FUNDS FOR RESEARCH AND DEVELOPMENT RELATING TO THE B–2 BOMBER AIRCRAFT. Of the unobligated balance of amounts appropriated for fiscal year 2011 for the Air Force and available for procurement of B–2 bomber aircraft modifications, post-production support, and other charges, $20,000,000 may be available for fiscal year 2012 for research, development, test, and evaluation with respect to a conventional mixed load capability for the B–2 bomber aircraft.

SEC. 135. AVAILABILITY OF FISCAL YEAR 2011 FUNDS TO SUPPORT ALTERNATIVE OPTIONS FOR EXTREMELY HIGH FREQUENCY TERMINAL INCREMENT 1 PROGRAM OF RECORD.

(a) IN GENERAL.—Of the unobligated balance of amounts appropriated for fiscal year 2011 for the Air Force and available for procurement of B–2 bomber aircraft modifications, post-production support, and other charges, $15,000,000 may be available to support alternative options for the extremely high frequency terminal Increment 1 program of record.

(b) PLAN TO SECURE PROTECTED COMMUNICATIONS.—Not later than 90 days after the date of the enactment of this Act, the Secretary of the Air Force shall submit to the congressional defense committees a plan to provide an extremely high frequency terminal for secure protected communications for the B–2 bomber aircraft and other aircraft.

TITLE II – Research, Development, Test, and Evaluation

Subtitle B – Program Requirements, Restrictions, and Limitations

SEC. 216. LIMITATION ON USE OF FUNDS FOR INCREMENT 2 OF B–2 BOMBER AIRCRAFT EXTREMELY HIGH FREQUENCY SATELLITE COMMUNICATIONS PROGRAM. Of the funds authorized to be appropriated by section 201 for research, development, test, and evaluation for the Air Force as specified in the funding table in section 4201 and available for Increment 2 of the B–2 bomber aircraft extremely high frequency satellite communications program, not more than 40 percent may be obligated or expended until the date that is 15 days after the date on which the Secretary of the Air Force submits to the congressional defense committees the following:

(1) The certification of the Secretary that—

(A) the United States Government will own the data rights to any extremely high frequency active electronically steered array antenna developed for use as part of a system to support extremely high frequency protected satellite communications for the B–2 bomber aircraft; and,

---

(B) the use of an extremely high frequency active electronically steered array antenna is the most cost effective and lowest risk option available to support extremely high frequency satellite Communications for the B–2 bomber aircraft.

(2) A detailed plan setting forth the projected cost and schedule for research, development, and testing on the extremely high frequency active electronically steered array antenna.

FY2013 Department of Defense Appropriations (S.Rept. 112-196: To accompany H.R. 5856)

Note: as of this writing, this legislation has not been passed into law.

Committee Initiatives: B–52 Combat Network Communications Technology

[CONECT].—The fiscal year 2013 budget request includes no funds in Aircraft Procurement, Air Force for the B–52 CONECT program of record due to the Air Force's decision to terminate the program, and $34,700,000 in Research, Development, Test and Evaluation, Air Force for a restructured, descoped B–52 CONECT program. The Committee understands that the Air Force is reviewing its decision to terminate the program of record in light of potential requirements of the Global Strike Command. The Committee further understands that should the Air Force reverse its decision to terminate B–52 CONECT during the fiscal year 2014 budget process, prior year funds would be available to reinstate the program following approval by the congressional defense committees. The Committee directs that no funds for B–52 CONECT program of record post-milestone C activities or a B–52 CONECT restructured program may be obligated or expended until 30 days after the congressional defense committees have been briefed on the Air Force's proposed way ahead, to include certification of full funding of the proposed program.

Committee Recommended Adjustments: B–52 Strategic Radar Replacement [SR2].—The Committee is aware the Air Force conducted a lengthy analysis of alternatives in 2011 to address a Strategic Radar Replacement [SR2] for the B–52H. The existing APQ–166 radar was produced in the 1960s, has a 20 to 30 hour mean-time between failure rate, and capability limitations. The Committee understands that the current APQ–166 radar is costly to operate and maintain. Therefore, the Committee encourages the Secretary of the Air Force to reconsider the decision to terminate the SR2 program.

FY2013 Department of Defense Authorizations (P.L. 112-239)

TITLE I – Procurement

Subtitle D – Air Force Programs

SEC. 142. RETIREMENT OF B–1 BOMBER AIRCRAFT.

(a) IN GENERAL.—Section 8062 of title 10, United States Code, is amended by adding at the end the following new subsection:

(h)(1) Beginning October 1, 2011, the Secretary of the Air Force may not retire more than six B–1 aircraft.

(2) The Secretary shall maintain in a common capability configuration not less than 36 B–1 aircraft as combat-coded aircraft.

(3) In this subsection, the term 'combat-coded aircraft' means aircraft assigned to meet the primary aircraft authorization to a unit for the performance of its wartime mission.''.

(b) CONFORMING AMENDMENT.—Section 132 of the National Defense Authorization Act for Fiscal Year 2012 (Public Law 112–81; 125 Stat. 1320) is amended by striking subsection (c).

In regards to the nuclear certification requirements of the Next-Generation Bomber, SEC. 211. states;

The Secretary of the Air Force shall ensure that the next-generation long-range strike bomber is—

capable of carrying strategic nuclear weapons as of the date on which such aircraft achieves initial operating capability; and

certified to use such weapons by not later than two years after such date.

TITLE II – Research, Development, Test, and Evaluation

Subtitle B – Program Requirements, Restrictions, and Limitations

SEC. 211. NEXT-GENERATION LONG-RANGE STRIKE BOMBER AIRCRAFT NUCLEAR CERTIFICATION REQUIREMENT. The Secretary of the Air Force shall ensure that the next generation long-range strike bomber is—

(1) capable of carrying strategic nuclear weapons as of the date on which such aircraft achieves initial operating capability; and

(2) certified to use such weapons by not later than two years after such date.

Author Contact Information

Jeremiah Gertler
Specialist in Military Aviation
jgertler@crs.loc.gov, 7-5107

Acknowledgments

Although subsequently maintained and updated by Jeremiah Gertler, this report was written by Lt. Col. (now Col.) Michael Miller, USAF, during his term as a fellow at CRS in 2012-2013.